Only Dead Fish Go with the Flow

Work smarter. Dream bigger.
Live an extraordinary life.

Darren McMahon

Only Dead Fish Go with the Flow

ISBN: 978-0-9910823-9-1

Published by Full Sail Publishing
Chicago, IL

FULL SAIL PUBLISHING

For Laura and Mila

CONTENTS

PREFACE

When I decided to take a nap, exhausted from studying for finals, I had no idea I might die.

On the 8th floor of the library at UC Santa Barbara, I pulled three chairs into a cubicle to form a cave of privacy and dozed off.

I woke up with no memory of what had happened, on an emergency-transport stretcher, paramedics rolling me to an elevator.

Later, I learned a couple of other students, studying in nearby cubicles, had heard me shaking uncontrollably on top of the chairs, rattling the dividers separating the cubicles. They'd tried to help me, but my body spasmed with uncontrollable convulsions. When my eyes rolled back in my head, they had called the paramedics.

Young, healthy, confident, strong, and maybe a little cocky, I chalked up this weird incident to too many late nights and long days, too much work condensed by student-athlete hours, and not enough play. Maybe too much junk food and a few bad college habits. I decided I'd be fine.

I was wrong.

It turned out life as I'd known it would never be the same.

For a while, things went on as they had before. Then, two years later, it happened again.

Now a senior in college, I felt great, on top of the world, dreaming of fun after-college plans and trying to decide my calling in life as I crammed for finals.

This time, I was in my apartment when the seizure hit. My roommate discovered me and called for help.

I woke up on the floor of my bedroom, in the dark, not knowing where I was or how I'd gotten there. A tunnel of light blinded me, and voices confused me. I had no idea what was happening. This was scary, disorienting stuff, but I seemed fine when it was over.

You'd think I might have been worried. And maybe I was, a little. But it was easy to chalk up this latest incident to the stress of finals and looming graduation. It happened a couple more times, then the seizures stopped.

For five or six years, life went back to normal. I traveled, worked odd jobs, and pondered what I genuinely wanted, trying to figure out my life purpose while putting the strange episodes behind me.

Then, in my late twenties and early thirties, the seizures happened again. Slowly at first, about once a year, they came, starting out as relatively minor. I handled them as I had before. Sure, they were scary, but I was okay. Just stressed and working too much.

Everything changed when I had a big seizure.

By now, it was the early 2000s. I had been riding high, turning myself into a millennial millionaire on paper, buying homes and renting them in California, Texas, and Nevada. Life was grand, and business was good until the bottom fell out of the real estate market in January 2008.

I wasn't sleeping well, operating under heavy stress. One night, at home with my girlfriend and an out-of-town friend who'd spent the night, I had a much more severe episode.

This time, I fell out of bed, shaking and sweating uncontrollably on the floor.

My girlfriend's crying and screaming revived me. "Wake up! Wake up, Darren!"

My eyes rolled back in my head, and my breathing became irregular. I saw a long tunnel and random lights. Voices came at me as if from a long distance away. I didn't know what was happening or where I was. I thought my time had come.

The lights grew brighter and the voices louder as I began to come around. When I finally opened my eyes again, paramedics hovered over me in my bedroom. My girlfriend cried on the shoulder of my friend, Sanjay.

One of the paramedics reassured me. "Darren, you're going be okay." He shined a flashlight in my eyes and asked me questions. "We need to take you to the hospital, but don't be alarmed," he said.

The next day, my girlfriend and Sanjay told me they'd thought I was gone. They said I'd stopped breathing for about two minutes after the seizure stopped. My skin had turned colors, my eyes rolled back, and my body was motionless even though sweat poured from my body. They'd been scared shitless.

Approximately a year later, while traveling with my girlfriend in North Carolina to do some furniture shopping, I had a pair of intense seizures while staying at a hotel. Again, I fell out of bed, and the paramedics were called. This time, they said I'd had a major episode followed by a second one before waking up. Things were getting serious.

Each time I experienced one of these episodes, it happened during a stressful period in my life while I slept. Compounding the confusion of waking up in the dark, on the floor, surrounded by yelling and crying people, a new set of fears was born. What if I injured myself falling out of bed? What if I didn't wake up at all the next time this happened? I was afraid to close my eyes, fearing it might be the last time I would be awake.

I underwent a series of tests to try to find the underlying cause of my seizures. Doctors found a form of epilepsy. The consensus is that these episodes were brought on by stress combined with a lack of sleep and proper rest.

I've been on medication for years now. Hopefully, that will change soon. Once I've gone without a seizure for over five years, I can have an advanced sleep EEG test that will determine if I can be weaned off medication at night. I haven't had a seizure for many years (knock wood) and will schedule the EEG soon.

Dealing with a major health issue or a brush with death is a potent wake-up call. It puts things in perspective and forces you to focus on what's important. In my case, my seizures turned out to be one of the best things that ever happened to me.

During the half-dozen years, when I didn't have any episodes, I took stock of my life and became more aware of the things I valued. In a way, having this condition awakened my spirit and got me started down a path that positively changed my life.

I realized how precious life is and how easily it might be taken away. I learned how to balance my work and personal time with greater harmony, and I am much more protective of my family time. I've found ways to become more peaceful and relax regularly, and I sleep like a baby these days. At the end of each day, I am grateful and pray for another day tomorrow.

Some folks don't get such a wake-up call until later in life or perhaps after it's too late—either they die or lose someone they love. All of us take things for granted to some degree. Often, we don't realize it until the hammer comes down unexpectedly, and everything changes.

I was lucky to receive such a powerful wake-up call and moved forward with a new purpose, focusing on achieving my dreams and inspiring others to do the same.

As I write, the Covid-19 pandemic is impacting the world, causing me to step back and press the pause/reflect button on my life. I was reminded that everything that seemed so urgent and important could disappear in the blink of an eye.

I am deeply empathetic toward the people who have either lost their lives or had to endure tremendous hardships and loss because of this deadly virus. It's been a horrible wake-up call for us all in countless ways. And it's also an opportunity.

Without such a sudden and unavoidable occurrence in my life, I would have continued running on autopilot, missing out on the priceless gems woven into every moment, and not even knowing it.

I passionately believe now is the time to reflect on the things that have been and have not been working. As a society, we must act together to become a cleaner, healthier, and more unified world. Leadership starts at an early age, and now is the time to call upon our younger generations to look outside themselves for ways to step up and face challenges head-on. Ultimately, it's up to all of us to wake up, learn from what we're going through, and pull together as a team, helping each other forge ahead into the unknown future.

This is one of my primary motivations for writing this book—to help people wake up, no seizure or catastrophe required.

All of us sleepwalk through life at times. We float, letting the tides take us where they will. For some, it might be a little catnap, going with the flow for short periods. For others, it may be a deep, drunken sleep on the edge of oblivion, adrift for much of the time. I awoke from my earlier self, grateful for each day of life, letting go of the past and my fears, and taking complete responsibility for creating the life of my dreams. My best life.

Believing everything happens for a reason, I decided my reason for surviving is you, the person who might benefit from reading my story and insights about building a successful life.

Do you tend to float through life, letting it happen to you? Do you fight the current every step of the way or plot a course and navigate your way, weathering storms and obstacles with confidence?

Have you dreamed of success, financial or otherwise, but have no idea how to achieve it? Or even how to get started? Do you believe success and fulfillment go hand in hand? Or have you lost faith? Has the path to happiness become unclear?

I'm here to tell you that with the right mindset, you can have the success of your dreams and be emotionally fulfilled and happy too.

In this book, I'll share my experiences and the key ingredients I used to completely transform my life and tackle it head-on. I'll share stories with you to show you what can be overcome, no matter where you are in life or how difficult things are for you right now.

I went from believing I had taken my last breath to waking with a condition I feared would kill me as I slept; from a medical mystery to a broke real estate investor, to finally creating the life I dreamed of. My finances, spirituality, contribution, health, vitality, and relationships are light-years ahead of where they were.

Now, I know there are no limits to what any of us can achieve in life. Most of us just need a little push. Consider me that push.

Expect a mixture of stories, information, inspiration, how-to steps, and exercises designed to get you onto the road to success and fulfillment and help you feel hopeful, motivated, and unstoppable.

I'm confident you will realize, as I did, that you already possess many of the tools you need to set a new course for yourself. You just need to open your mind and your heart to see them and put them to work for you.

There's no reason not to have a life filled with success, fulfillment, and happiness. So, let's make it happen!

CHAPTER 1

Attitude

In the depth of winter, I finally learned that there was in me an invincible summer.

Albert Camus

Sunshine streamed through the clouds as the yacht slipped through the crystal-clear water of a Norwegian fjord. At the back of the yacht, gentle waves rippled toward the horizon.

I stared in awe at the sheer cliffs and waterfalls as water

cascaded down the lush mountainside, and springtime proudly displayed itself. A flood of emotions and memories overwhelmed me—gratitude, pride, satisfaction, and emotional fulfillment. I smiled, thinking back to what seemed like only yesterday when I'd been an unfocused ski bum and waiter who'd scoured the Salvation Army and Goodwill stores for clothes. Back then, I had no real career and no idea what my purpose was in the world.

My wife Laura snuggled up to me, looping an arm around my waist as I shook the memories of times past from my head. "Love, our flight leaves in three days for Stockholm, but I'm not sure I want to leave this place," she said.

"No worries, Laura." I smiled. "Let's just continue to enjoy this amazing landscape. Everything will work out as it is meant to."

We hugged one another close, and I knew this was a magical moment I'd never forget. I closed my eyes as a tremendous sense of gratitude washed over me. My life had truly come full circle, and the new, real me was a mere remnant of my previous self.

The yacht slowly came to a stop at a tiny town. Looking down at the glassy, blue water again, I saw my reflection almost like a dream. My thoughts raced back to the days when I had lacked focus. I asked myself what had changed, searching for the beginning moments of the shift that had led to this dream life. The answer was clear–my attitude had changed!

Three days later, 500 beautiful pictures later, I boarded a plane for my next adventure in Sweden with my wife, feeling successful in my own skin, having finally realized what it meant to be emotionally fulfilled. My work/life balance was in check, and my life was right where I wanted it to be. And it had all started with my attitude.

Attitude is Everything

I'm a "the glass is half full" kind of guy. Realizing this choice is relative (and that I could write a whole chapter on this glass-fullness conundrum alone), I make a conscious choice to see the gift in the glass *itself.*

When it comes to life, if you choose positive language and a positive attitude over other options, you're far more likely to be successful. I like those odds.

To stack the odds more in your favor, focus on the words you use and your thought patterns. These have the most impact on our attitude. If you routinely say things like "Woe is me" or ask questions like "Why are terrible things always happening to me?", you're stacking the deck against yourself. You will experience a more challenging, negative life simply because you keep reinforcing these damaging messages. After a while, your brain and your repeated thoughts fuse. Now your brain tells you your thoughts are facts, and that's hard because you can't experience the joy of life when you're focused on the stories you're telling yourself about the way things "are."

You don't have to be stuck here because we're all blessed with the ability to evaluate our thoughts and change them for the better. In any given situation, we choose our attitude, and our attitude influences our choices, feelings, and actions. So, managing your attitude is essential to controlling your outcomes. Everyone knows that. But how do we harness this ability we all have to affect our attitudes in ways that help us?

Start by reframing your thoughts and words in a positive light and surrounding yourself with positive, enlightening people, and your chances for success go way up.

Negative thinking can be a hard habit to break, so let's look closer at what you can do to kickstart your positive attitude.

The attitude/dream connection

Having a poor attitude spreads across all areas of your life like cancer, destroying everything it touches. Not only will people not want to help or be around the negative version of you, but you won't have the energy to put in the hours necessary to get things done because a bad attitude saps your energy and steals your motivation. You won't want to do the legwork required to accomplish anything. Heck, you may not even want to get out of bed in the morning. On the days you do, you could find yourself walking through life on autopilot, growing more negative as a result. Before you know it, a negative thought-spiral can drag you down to the point where even your dreams seem silly. That's when most people begin to float through life, doing what they can, when they can, and little else.

The good news is that you don't have to live this way. You can keep your dreams alive by boosting your attitude, focusing on the basics of a good attitude outlined in the next section.

I've always been a dreamer. Because I had such a powerful desire to make things happen, I believed I had a good attitude by default and was surprised to discover that, while desire is important and feeds into attitude, it is only part of the equation.

Each of the following elements works together to create a domino-like effect on your thought patterns. After you've reviewed the list below, spend time thinking of when you've excelled in these areas. This will add to the positive balance in your attitude stores. Also, ask yourself what you can do to stimulate growth in these areas so you can enjoy immediate results. I'll give you some suggestions at the end of this chapter, but first, let's look at the main building blocks of a successful attitude.

Key Ingredients in Successful Attitudes

Desire

It is essential to have desire as desire develops passion. Desire acts as a driver to keep you moving forward even when you get knocked down and feel discouraged. Powerful desire is like having fuel in the tank to keep your engine running and your fire burning no matter how long it takes to reach your destination or how rough your journey.

Persistence

Your ability to get up after you've been knocked down and to keep going even when the going gets rough sets the stage for success. Your willingness to do whatever it takes is what gets every job done.

Daily, I use thoughtful gifts given to me by my pals, Mark Vukelich and Sam Wegert, as reinforcement anchors to remind me of who I am and of the persistence and qualities I stand for. Mark's gift was a little drinking cup I keep in my bathroom with the Chinese proverb "Fall seven times, stand up eight" inscribed on it. This philosophy has certainly been tested over time! Sam's gift was a coffee cup with a personalized message. I use it in the mornings while eating breakfast. The message reads, "Thank you, Darren, for being an amazing mentor and a tremendous inspiration for me. Your ambitious, competitive, and resilient spirit is very admirable. I really appreciate our relationship." Reading such messages consistently from Mark and Sam helps me stay the course and be true to who I am.

Reflect on times when you've persisted through adversity and triumphed. Doing so will subconsciously reinforce your belief in yourself and fan the flames of desire. Further encourage persistence by finding your own daily reinforcements, whether they are inspiring inscriptions on items you regularly use or they come from other sources.

Creativity

Seeing opportunities where others don't, and thinking creatively, will set you apart and help you keep going when it seems like all hope is lost.

Every challenge you face presents an opportunity for

learning and advancement. Embrace that idea, and become the person who, when others get stuck or give up, picks up the ball and keeps moving.

Creativity brings new perspectives and energy to any situation. Being creative means being flexible and dynamic in your views and having the vision to see possibilities. Coupled with a willingness to implement innovative ideas, a solution is inevitable for any problem when you bring creativity to the table. It is largely through creativity that I have sold approximately 100 million dollars in my medical sales career.

Vision

Vision allows you to see beyond where you are, to the horizon in your mind, even when you are down in the trenches with your sleeves rolled up, sweating, and toiling away in the dust and dirt with no end in sight.

It is vital to keep your eyes on your goals, exercising tremendous focus.

Remember, your destination is a journey, often over many bumpy roads. With a vision of where you want to go, you can reverse engineer your goals and make them a reality. We'll talk more about this later. First, let's look at a few enemies of desire, persistence, creativity, and vision and how to beat them.

The Blame Game

Nothing saps desire and stalls creativity and vision while stopping forward progress as fast as blame can. Blame even makes us feel justified for a crappy attitude, blind to what our mindset is taking from us. People who play the blame game are never emotionally fulfilled and are never successful because they've created the habit of not taking responsibility for their actions. This is just one slippery ride away from not taking responsibility for their attitude either.

Do you ever arrive late for a meeting and blame your lateness on the traffic or the weather? You're playing the blame game. Traffic is a part of life. Getting a late start or not accounting for potential delays is on you, not the traffic.

Take a hard look at yourself to spot and get rid of this harmful pattern if you find it lurking in your thoughts. Get tough with yourself, even about seemingly minor thoughts. Don't justify them even when you're confident something or someone else can be blamed. Instead, look at what you might have done differently and take responsibility for your outcomes. Ask the hard questions and stay in a place that gives you the power to move ahead in positive ways instead of floundering in negativity, propped up by excuses. Tap into your creativity and desire to shift your thinking to positive solutions and away from energy-sucking blame or regret.

Make it your policy not to shift responsibility. Do it to keep yourself on track and keep the creeping effects of negative self-talk away from your positive attitude. Buck-up and shoulder the load. People around you will have more respect for you, even when you make a mistake, if you take responsibility and present solutions, not complaints. The admiration and respect from others will bolster your attitude too.

Small Changes That Conquer Excuses

Change one thing.

When trying to change any behavior, start by altering one small thing to start.

I used to run in just-in-time mode. I would show up to a meeting or an event, and my butt would hit the seat as the lights went down. Routinely pushing it to the last minute and cutting it close was my habit. I usually blamed traffic. It wasn't until I took a hard look at how this negatively affected my internal landscape that I committed to being the guy who gets places early. What a difference this one thing has made to my life. And anyone can do it.

If you are perpetually tardy, how late are you? Most of us have a pattern. I was a five-minute late person. Maybe you usually run about fifteen minutes late. Just leave that much earlier for every appointment, and you'll seldom be late again. If you end up being massively early and alone, use the time to read, send a text to someone you care about, or prepare for the meeting ahead, so you are mentally focused and ready to roll.

Shift your focus.

Careless is a beautifully exact word. I *care less* about you than I do for myself. By shifting your perspective and focusing on other people, you show care and respect for them in any situation.

When you are late for a meeting or an appointment, it reflects a level of selfishness and carelessness, whether you mean to or not. Lateness tells others you don't care about their time as much as yours.

Arriving a few minutes early or on-time shows people you appreciate their time. It may not seem like much, but punctuality is a sticking point for many people, and most people tend to remember how others behave.

Serving others

In addition to shifting your focus to others, take it one step farther and commit yourself to the service of others.

Most people tend to serve themselves. I'm no exception and have gone through periods in my life where I looked out primarily for me, me, me. After years of struggles and challenges, something magic happened. I began to embrace how good it felt to help people. This happened approximately seventeen years ago when I began volunteering at personal development seminars. I tuned in to the positive energy I received from my interactions with others at these events. Serving others made me feel better about myself while I reaped the overflowing goodness of other's appreciation. I was, in fact, serving myself by serving others! Except in this scenario, everybody won. Go figure.

Attitude Creates Miracles

When I was in eighth grade, I was blessed to win various athletic rewards, including one of two given at our middle school for the top two athletes. There were two brackets, one for the bigger guys and one for the smaller ones. I was a little guy, not even five feet tall, tipping the scales at a whopping seventy-five pounds. My legs made up much of my body. I was a scrawny, little, athletic runt who loved competing.

My dad and grandfather, Papa, were tremendous supporters of my development as an athlete and came to as many games as possible. Dad coached a season for my baseball team with my best friend David Wells' Dad. David lived next door to me. We were almost identical clones of each other and the same size and skill level in the sports we competed in. The only difference was that David was a sailor, and I was a skier.

Despite my small size, I was a good athlete with solid, fundamental skills and a gift for playing most sports. In high school, I tried out for three of my favorite sports—basketball, soccer, and baseball. During the first week, due to my spirit as a little hustler, I led the running drills in the tryouts for each sport. I felt energized and excited as well as confident I would make the teams with my friends who had played with me before on all-star, select traveling teams. My attitude was at the top of its game; I was ready for high school sports!

After running try-outs for three days in each sport, the coaches posted lists of people who had made the team and those who hadn't. My name was scratched off the list in all three sports. I was crushed and angry. I hadn't even had a chance to prove myself by playing a position or doing any competitive drills to show my skills. To make matters worse, the friends I'd played various sports with in middle school all made the teams while I was left out in the cold.

The exact same thing happened in my sophomore year. It was like horrible deja vu. After the first week, I was cut from all three of my favorite sports. Again, I felt rejected, angry, sad, disappointed, and rocked even harder at my core. My identity up until then had been of a sporty, little guy who everyone loved and wanted on their team. After two years of cuts and rejection, I wasn't so sure about anything.

Casting a large shadow over the whole experience was my parents' marriage breaking up. Getting knocked down once or twice is one thing but failing six times while dealing with my crumbling family life felt like too much to bear. At the time, I didn't have the personal development skills to manage the emotional swirl and ensuing identity crisis I had to endure. I was at an all-time low.

Fortunately, I was the product of two strong-willed parents whom I loved dearly. When my parents divorced between 8th grade and freshman year of high school, I went to live with my mother as part of the custody agreement. Mom had an incredibly positive attitude despite her challenges. She was my biggest fan and a huge support during these dark teenage times. She encouraged me to re-direct my focus and emotional energies into other sports where my size and abilities could be maximized and appreciated. Even though these other sports weren't my first (second or third) choices, I was grateful for an opportunity to take part in something.

I got involved in martial arts and went into Kuk Sool Won. This traditional Korean martial art is a systematic study of all the traditional fighting arts. I discovered the training was as much about developing my mind as it was about strengthening my body and physical skills. My small size was now helpful. With newfound confidence and determination to excel, I embraced my study of Kuk Sool Won and became a black belt in my senior year.

It was exciting to use my athletic background on the tumbling aspect of this martial art on a demonstration team that performed aerial tricks like backflips and front flips over many rows of kids. Learning how to do aerial tricks and maneuver my body inspired me to transition these skills to the snow, where I taught myself how to jump off hills and do flips and jumps.

Although it wouldn't have been my first pick either, I also became involved in track and field in my sophomore year and quickly excelled despite my tiny stature. Track was not something my heart was into, but I decided to make the most of the chance I'd been given. In junior year, I won many meets and the Marin County district for high hurdles (which must have been very funny to watch since the obstacles looked almost as tall as me). As a senior, I won the long jump for the district but could not defend my title in the high hurdles because I was accidentally bumped in the finals race by another competitor, forcing me to not even finish the race.

Though my identity took quite a beating the first few years of high school, I learned who I am isn't tied to any one sport. I learned I was blessed with a God-given talent to excel in many sports and many areas of my life. I decided if any one thing didn't work out, I would keep trying and move to the next until I found something that did. I decided I wasn't going to let anyone else's thoughts or beliefs about me define who I am as a person; this is a choice left to me!

This became the chapter of my life where my conviction about personal responsibility began. Whatever I chose to do, I knew it would be up to me to succeed. I learned it was not worth my time and energy to play the blame game or mope around when things didn't go my way. If I got knocked down seven times, I got up eight.

This philosophy served me well by shifting my focus to new conquests and away from the negative swirl of feelings that had tried to drag me down earlier. My positive attitude helped me become a black belt, win district titles in track, attend college, and compete at that level, and earn my degree. These experiences (the good and the seemingly bad) helped mold and shape me into the person I am today.

Perhaps God gave me this series of tests to inspire me to become the best person I could be at an early age, while I was still easily capable of change if I tried. These events might have been a higher calling to help other people by sharing my story and giving them tools to help shape who they are too. That's the cool thing about an optimistic, positive attitude—anything is possible.

Challenging Life Experiences

Help yourself as you face your own challenges by asking quality questions to uncover different perspectives on what's happening. For example, ask yourself, "What's the blessing in this situation? How can this situation serve me right now?"

I choose to believe every situation we face can serve us and propel us to new heights. Everything is a seed for something greater to come, provided we have the right attitude and mindset to gain these valuable insights.

It's all about the questions you ask and how you choose to look at life's challenges. If you ask debilitating questions like "Why is this always happening to me?", you're going to get negative answers and thought swirls that lead to a lack of positive results, keeping you stuck.

Be careful where you place your focus and about the questions you ask yourself because you will get precisely what you focus on.

Examples of some fabulous questions that will serve and not hinder you are the following:

- What is amazing about this problem or situation right now?
- How can this serve and inspire me today and in the future?
- How can I learn from this challenge?
- How can I use this gift to be the best version of me?

Heart and Desire are Mighty

Early on, I learned the importance of not judging a book by its cover or feeling as if I know someone upon first meeting them. Though I've been guilty of this behavior many times, I've also learned that you don't know anyone else's story at first glance or understand why they are who they are until you get to know them.

Many people judge others by their title or by their status on social media. Credentials and numbers of followers don't equate to value, character, success, or fulfillment. Focus instead on a person's authenticity, genuineness, and the fundamentals of their real character. What one may lack in title and status can be more than offset by their strong internal desire and tenaciousness. Fancy titles and social media posts are often facades that reveal only the highlights of who a person really is. They are like masks people wear to portray themselves in the best light. So, I look deeper and hope others do the same for me.

Judging people is not only a weak position to take where others are concerned, but it also deprives you too. People who judge often feel superior to the people they are judging. They cut others off at the stem and believe they walk the moral high ground. By doing this, they deprive themselves of the opportunity to get to know people. Limiting what we learn, not finding out what others have to offer, serves no one.

Posturing

In the personal development space, I've learned about the importance of posturing when it comes to meeting people. There are three positions you can use—superior, equal, and inferior. Each position reflects the level of experience or the stance you wish to take with another person. Whether we acknowledge these positions consciously or not, we all take them, so why not make the best choice?

For example, if you were to take a superior position with someone, you might come across as highly knowledgeable and experienced like an expert. If the person you are speaking to is superior in this regard, you might connect right away. If they are not attempting to be superior, you might portray a bit of arrogance, superiority, or a been-there-done-that, I-don't-have-time-for-this attitude, which may put them off or make them feel like you are judging them. Maybe you are.

Judgment and ego often go hand in hand. Judgers often need to feel superior to compensate for their own insecurity. Maybe they don't have the education or experience to back up their superior stance, so they pretend. It doesn't take long to figure this phony posturing out, so don't fall into that trap. Instead, focus on being genuine, regardless of where you stand.

We all have our strengths and areas where we can learn more. If you're not sure about a given topic, ask questions, and listen to others' answers. As the old saying goes, "It is better to remain silent and thought the fool than to open your mouth and remove all doubt."

When I meet new people, I like to come from an equal position and occasionally an inferior position and work my way up. I ask lots of questions and try to let the other person do most of the talking as I am genuinely interested in them. As things begin to unfold, I get a better picture of who they are and how our relationship could develop.

Working toward equal posture is the best place to be for everyone. Well-balanced people know life is often give and take and that there is something to be learned from everyone.

Sometimes, the best examples of well-balanced attitudes and thoughtful approaches to success in life come from people you know well. My friend, Jeff Butler, embodies the best success attitude of anyone I know. He's one of the top sales executives for the Fortune eight company McKesson and feels success is not about him.

"Success is how others I serve benefit from my service. Whether it's customers, family members, colleagues, or friends, if their lives are better because of my interaction with them or my service to them, then that's a success for me. Success is not defined by something personal; it's defined by the betterment of others in my life," Jeff said.

In addition to Jeff's positive spirit and attitude, I admire his devotion to philanthropy and his rock-solid work ethic. To date, Jeff has twelve children. Ten of them are adopted. Each year, he devotes his time to building schools in Ethiopia where eight of his adopted children are from, running Mission 1:27, a non-profit organization that supports these efforts.

Jeff believes maintaining a positive attitude is a choice, not a feeling. "It's choosing where to focus despite your varying circumstances throughout the day." To do this, Jeff reviews a list every day that reflects his key ingredients for a positive attitude. He calls the list FOCUS.

- F stands for faith (in God, the foundation, and core). F also stands for family, friends, fitness, and finances.

- O stands for one moment at a time, one thing at a time, and one day at a time. Whatever you do, spend your energy and time in the moment.

- C stands for confidence. Confidence is a precious commodity that comes and goes, but without it, you cannot do anything.

- U is one of the most important and stands for uncomfortable. You cannot choose anything in life without some level of discomfort. Comfort is what prevents us from pursuing our goals and dreams. Check in with yourself regularly to gauge your comfort. If you're not feeling discomfort, you're not pushing yourself.

- S is serving. Serving is the joy of life. When you are serving, you will find your purpose. Always look for ways to serve other people in different roles.

Jeff developed an incredible work ethic by watching his father work three jobs to support his family and during his time in the military. "My father had an incredibly strong work ethic and dedication to what he was doing. The military taught me that it's not always about you; it's about working as a team and the vital role you play in the bigger picture. There's no secret to success. It's about getting up early every day and working hard, staying focused, and being consistent in your efforts."

Jeff believes attitude is tied to thoughts. "All of us struggle with what I call stinking thinking. Make a choice to be mindful of your thoughts. If your attitude is down, it's because you are caught up in a swirl of stinking thinking. Much of life is all about perspective. Jeff and I have talked a lot about perspective and some of the challenges in our careers when it would have been easy to get negative and blame the outside world. Emotions go up and down every day. You can choose to think differently about things and take a new perspective when times are tough and you're feeling down. There's nothing easy about what I'm saying here. It's like working out; there is nothing easy about staying in shape or going to the gym. Like many things in life, your attitude takes daily work and application to see positive results."

The Magical "Why" Attitude

One of the most important questions you can ask yourself is, "What would I do if I knew I could not fail?" Think about what you genuinely want and why it is important to you. We'll come back to this again and again throughout this book because as you begin to move toward your goals and dreams, a clear picture of your dreams and your reasons for achieving them (your "why") will support you when the going gets tough. Your why will prop you up, carry you forward, and serve as a positive reminder of why it's worth it to do what you do. It's also difficult to get lost in negative headspace when you are thinking of your dreams and all the reasons you want to achieve them.

Figuring out what you want is essential to your success because you will find what drives you and makes you happy. You might discover this is not financial success. Perhaps you want emotional fulfillment and inner peace more than anything else. Maybe you value contribution to your community or want a life of continued learning and exploration. The wonderful thing about what drives each of us and makes us happy is how individual these things are. There are no right answers and no wrong ones. There is only what is true for you.

I know people who are rich on paper but poor internally and others who are rich in spirit but poor on paper. Most of us would like a harmonious balance of spiritual and monetary wealth.

Money can't buy you happiness, but it does provide you with options and opportunities. Without money, you may find yourself struggling to meet your basic needs and be distracted from finding your true calling. Being emotionally fulfilled and peaceful might be better if you had to choose one or the other.

If you struggle with getting in touch with what you want most in life and why, ask yourself what you value above money. It seems to me that people who have little materially but are rich in spirit, family, and relationships are closer to living a harmonious life than those who are materially wealthy but empty on the inside. Still, without the necessary resources, life can be challenging. So why not have both?

Before we move on to the next chapter, review the

following keys and tools that will help you develop and keep the attitude it takes to achieve an ideal state of being.

I suggest you use a notebook to record ideas and thoughts as you read each chapter and complete various assignments. Studies show writing what you've learned dramatically increases learning and absorption.

Schedule any action items or tasks for yourself as you go. Ask yourself what you can do this week to incorporate these keys and tools into your life.

Keys:

Daily reminders

Read these as you start your day to set yourself and your attitude up for success. Come up with your own list and keep the positive vibes flowing. These are also useful mantras to remember when negative thoughts creep into your day.

Life is a gift every day. Don't ever take it for granted. Life is unpredictable, so embrace uncertainty. Love life and learn to smile in the face of a chaotic world every day. This is a must, not a should. The chaos will always be there, and it is an opportunity and a gift given to us so we can learn how to dance with it every day. A life that is flatlining is boring and represents death, so embrace chaos and let it build you up.

Friendships are precious, especially the deeply connected ones where you share similar values. Guard them well and strive to tell at least one person daily how much you care for them. Genuine care or love for someone does not get old if you are consistent, assuming your actions are in sync with your words.

Ask yourself if what you are doing is getting you closer to what you truly need (not just what you want). People often sacrifice what they actually need to satisfy their immediate desires and wants. For example, if someone wants to lose weight but cannot refuse the temptation of putting their hand in the cookie jar, they aren't going to be happy in the end.

Be humble and perform random acts of kindness. Strive for one a day and make it a habit. This could be something as small as smiling at a stranger and saying hello, buying coffee for the person behind you in line, pumping someone's gas, or giving sincere compliments to people you don't know. Visit a hospital or a retirement facility and spend time with an elderly person who has no family. Become a big brother or big sister by volunteering with Big Brothers Big Sisters of America.

The opportunities to make a difference are endless. Something that may seem small to us can make a world of difference to someone else. Do something that resonates with you.

Check your life's priorities every week to become more consistent with who you are (or would like to be) as a person. If your priorities are out of alignment, you'll be miserable in your own skin. Take stock regularly by making a list of your priorities. For example, my priorities are faith in God, my awesome family, my close friends, my career, and associates who I might see every now and then or haven't had the pleasure of meeting yet.

Though I suggest being selective about who is in your inner circle, I am finding more regular friends becoming close friends as we attract people who share many of the same core values and similar missions in life. We propel each other to be the best, most inspired versions of ourselves, truly making a difference.

Have fun! Embrace fears and challenges as they will

always come and are meant to serve us and make our hearts sputter. Be thankful for the joy in everything else.

Visualize achieving through resilience. The only people who don't have any fear are six feet under!

Be good to others.

The golden rule will always serve you. Don't judge. Focus on rising to equal posture with people, and don't be afraid to come from an inferior position to let others shine. Let them talk. You listen. Think of what you might learn by keeping your mouth shut most of the time.

Be good to yourself.

Before we can love and appreciate others, we must learn to appreciate and love ourselves. Treat yourself like the golden goose who supplies everything you need to live a productive and harmonious life. Without yourself, you truly have nothing. Make sure to make emotional deposits in your own account first. If the plane is going down, put on your oxygen mask first, then help others. It's tough to help others if your tank is empty, so love yourself first!

Focus on gratitude for your blessings, and don't compare yourself to others.

It's more beneficial to be happy with what you have and with who you are than to continually pursue things you don't have or compare yourself to others. Although the grass may seem greener in your neighbor's yard, your neighbor might feel differently. They could be unhappy with their grass and feel hollow inside, despite their outward appearance. Who knows? What are you grateful for today?

Mind your own business.

If you are tempted to compare yourself and what you've accomplished to others, stop. Take a deep breath and refocus. Comparisons like these are a mistake, and here's why—you can't compare apples and oranges equally. Everyone has their own story, their own unique experiences, and circumstances. Who others are and what they've done is outside your control and none of your business.

Focus on what you can learn from others and on your own tasks rather than wasting time and energy thinking about things that don't concern you.

When you are open and genuinely believe there is something to be learned from every person you meet, the doors of opportunity are always open.

 **Tools:**

Strengthen your resolve and develop a belief system to bolster your best attitude. Use these tools to get the ball rolling.

- **Spend five minutes every morning expressing gratitude.** Journal, meditate, or just spend time thinking about or expressing thanks for your life's blessings.

- **Read books or listen to audiobooks** to regularly surround yourself with a positive, fulfilling peer group. Disassociate from negative people or those who don't support your vision and dreams.

- **Just say yes.** Years ago, my good friend, Rock Thomas (one of the most inspiring people I know and a tremendous transformational trainer), taught me to start saying yes when opportunities present themselves, knowing everything will fall into place. Try it and get off the procrastination train like a winner, overcoming your fear of failure, knowing there is growth in taking risks.

If, when an opportunity arises, your first thought is, "Wow! That sounds amazing!" but the thoughts that follow your initial excitement ask pesky questions or put up roadblocks and objections, just say yes anyway. You'll be glad you did.

- **Ask yourself, "What do I truly need to feel successful?"** Remember that money without fulfillment or happiness is not a good scenario and has tricked many people in the past. Write your goals in your notebook and take time to visualize them. Next, write all the reasons why you deserve everything you desire and the ways you are dedicating yourself to making your dreams a reality.

- **Remind yourself that success and**

fulfillment are not just for others; they are for you too! After I started asking myself, "Why not me?" I came up with so many answers that resonated with me that this exercise became much easier.

- **Stop focusing on being a victim**. This never serves us. Sometimes, things don't go our way (or so it may seem); however, everything that happens is happening *for* us, not *to* us. This is an especially important message for people who think they are not good enough or feel jinxed when it comes to getting what they genuinely want out of life. Remember, success is found on the other side of defeat. Know every apparent failure molds us for future success if we have the right attitude.

- **Visualize.** Imagine what you want and describe it in detail to yourself. What do you see, hear, and feel when you imagine achieving what you want? Having a passionate attitude toward your goals will take you far. Whenever I do anything, I think about and visualize a positive outcome. I believe a great result and my desired outcome are already in my grasp. My actual results may not be perfect, but they are always in the ballpark. This works the same way it does for a basketball player who bounces the ball three times at the free-throw line, visualizing the ball leaving their hand in a smooth arc and falling through the basket. Nothing but net. Visualizing uses all the senses. The same ballplayer not only sees the ball going in, but they hear the swish of the net, smell the leather of the basketball, and hear the roar of the crowd and the rumble of the building as the fans jump to their feet.

- **Incantations.** Utilize "I am" statements. I am unstoppable. I am courageous. I am love. These identity statements can be made in the morning, in the shower, in the car, or at night before you go to bed. Whenever feels right for you. It helps to find a time each day that works and do them as consistently as possible. Use your whole physiology and get your body involved. Stand up and pump out your chest with a fist pump and loudly say, "I am unstoppable!" I do this three times, but you choose whatever works for you. It helps to make sure your body movements and tone of voice fit the incantation. You might not loudly yell, "I am love!" with a fist pump. Instead, you might place your palms together and look into a mirror as you say this from your heart. Try different things. Switch it up and repeat the ones that feel the best or fit most with the attitude you are developing and nurturing at any given time.

CHAPTER 2

Modeling and Replicating

A good example has twice the value of good advice.

Albert Schweitzer

Anyone living the life of their dreams is always surrounded by peers and people who support them. Unless you have a positive attitude, it's going to be tough to attract people who want to help and support you because they are not going to want to be around you.

As Jim Rohn once said, "You are the average of the five people you spend the most time with." Make yourself a good part of those numbers.

Take an honest look at the five people you spend the most time with. Are they propelling you forward, challenging you, and inspiring you to expand and grow? If not, find a new tribe.

No matter what you want to do, you can be sure many successful and fulfilled people are already doing it. Most want to pass the torch and share their wisdom. One browse of YouTube will give you millions of examples of people demonstrating all kinds of things, eager to share their knowledge.

Learning how to change a tire from a stranger on the internet is one thing, but many people balk at the idea of approaching experts in real life. Let's change that by breaking down the steps and logic behind the fast-lane to success—modeling and replicating.

Modeling and replicating is the process of studying the habits of successful people and copying what they did to get where they are, mastering the fundamentals they're using, then adding your spin on their methods to make them your own. This process allows you to replicate successful processes without having to waste a lot of time. It's like kicking off your bike's training wheels one day and winning the Indy500 the next day. Okay, maybe not that fast, but you get the idea. Why stay in the slow lane when you can zip ahead with the best of them? Success leaves clues, so there is no reason to waste a lot of time.

Focus on Others' Success and Guarantee Your Own.

The key to effective modeling and replicating is finding people who are successful, emotionally fulfilled, and living an authentic and balanced life. Follow their example and start by adopting the fundamentals and routines they use. Once you have a solid foundation and have mastered the basics, you can tweak things to your liking.

This can be challenging for many people who want to immediately change things or who reject the processes of other people (usually because of ego or fear). There's something vulnerable about starting out with no knowledge. Most humans find this is an uncomfortable place to be. This goes all the way back to our primal need to protect ourselves by appearing strong in a group. Knowing this, and laughing at it even, can help us shed our caveman instincts so we can get to the business of learning.

You will get farther when you approach others from an equal or inferior position and let them guide you. Before you start the learning process, make a deal with yourself to ask questions, keep your mouth shut, listen to what they have to offer, and implement your chosen mentor's methods exactly as they describe. Know that when you do this, you will earn respect and not waste anyone's time, including your own. Thinking it through in advance will help quiet those voices in your head that might try to steer the simple process into a ditch, derailing you.

If you're still having a tough time with the idea of following someone else's methods, know that you will also offer to assist your mentor, helping them build their business and returning the favor. Not only will this reciprocation soothe your ego, but it also supports your positive attitude and reminds you to be humble and prepared to give back as much as you can in any situation.

It also helps to consider the value of working with a top dog. What you might learn from your chosen teacher could cost tens of thousands of dollars in college education. Studying for a degree never gives you such detailed, job-specific tools either. When you look at it this way, why wouldn't you leverage the knowledge and experience of successful people within your own company or field of choice?

You'd be surprised at how many people balk at the idea of approaching successful people to ask for guidance. Don't be afraid to be different. In fact, dare to be different. If you think like most people, you'll get common results. That's not what we're after, so let's knock down the biggest hurdles between our mentors and us.

Squashing the Fear of Approaching Successful People

Successful people aren't too busy to help you. The people who fit our model for the best to learn from are successful, emotionally fulfilled, and living an authentic and balanced life. These are the kind of people who love giving back. They are probably surprised more people don't approach them. That doesn't mean you won't run into people who appear too busy to mentor you.

Most successful people are driven, maximizing their time each day. This can reinforce the idea that they'd never have time for you. Accept that someone might not have time to work with you now because they are focused on their goals or projects. Be patient and willing to wait. Don't get discouraged. The important thing is to step up to the plate, serious about what you are asking for. Be humble and flexible, and let them know when the time is right for them, you'll be focused, grateful, and prepared to give 100% to your time together.

When you sit down with your chosen mentor, come prepared with questions. Don't assume anything. Ask! Ask good questions and listen to the answers you receive. This skill, more than any other, will help you learn the most. Take notes. A yellow pad and pen, ready to go, is a sign that you are serious about what others have to say.

Be a Gift

When you ask people for help, you're allowing them to give back, not being a burden to them. You're helping them become even more powerful and emotionally fulfilled. By asking someone for their thoughts and methods, you validate them as a human being and let them know they matter. When you decide someone is too busy or not interested in helping you, so you don't ask them for help, you deprive them of opportunities.

Successful people have found success, in part, because they believed in something. They put their hearts and souls into their work. Maybe they've been at it for a long time and are beginning to slow down and divert their energy into other areas. Then, here you come, willing to carry their torch and spread their message, putting energy into the world in a positive way on their behalf. Who wouldn't want that? So, ask away. Shift from thinking of yourself as a burden to knowing you are a gift and go help someone as they help you.

How to Find the Best Role-Models

Start by going online and searching for the best people in your industry. Find out who the leaders are. Check out industry magazines and read about the top people in your field of interest. Look around your company too. Maybe someone there exemplifies everything you'd like to be. Accept that you might have to look farther afield to find someone truly at the top of their game.

Once you have a handful of names, send out notes, and find out what it will take to spend a few minutes together talking about their world and how they got to where they are. Offer to buy them a cup of coffee or take them to lunch but promise not to take up too much of their time as this is one of their most precious commodities.

Although tweets, texts, and emails seem to dominate today, I highly encourage you to stand out from the crowd. Handwritten letters or notes can take you a long way. People are busy and may get hundreds of texts, tweets, emails, and voice mails each day. A return phone call may not happen unless you call dozens of times and risk being a pest. A handwritten letter or note stands out. Don't underestimate the power of this. When you consider the amount of time and effort you might put into saving time with a text, the payoff from a handwritten note makes it a much more efficient place to start.

Don't get discouraged if there is no reply to your first

handwritten note. The best role models are remarkably busy, appropriately managing their time. Be creative. Consider sending a small gift for simply taking the time to consider meeting with you. In some industries, one cannot do this due to laws. Even in situations where gifts are allowed, most people don't do this, so dare to be different. Your results will, most likely, pleasantly surprise you.

Time is Money.

When I began in the corporate sales world, I knew who the top salespeople were as the company made it extremely easy for everyone to know where they ranked. I was near dead last.

I started off doing things my way, not using the approach of the most successful account executives. I had a lot of energy, and in a bull-headed fashion, I went into medical office buildings and, starting on the top floor, knocked on every door, working my way down.

I thought, "This is a big building with so many offices. I'm bound to build my business and land some clients." And I did. I added many smaller clients to my book of business. They consumed much of my time and penny-pinched every item we sold. In hindsight, most did not seem to value the programs or services I brought to the table.

Later, I learned the most successful reps focused their efforts on the top 20% of their clients because those clients produced 80% of their business. They were smart with their time management and didn't spin their wheels spending energy with tiny accounts that consumed all their precious time.

I ignored the proven success formula called the Pareto 80-20 rule the top sales executives knew and lived by. Instead, I spent 80% of my time on accounts that produced only 20% of my results and sales. This was backward. Something was missing.

I divided my accounts into A, B, and C accounts. A accounts were my top accounts, where 80% of my time should be spent according to the Pareto 80-20 rule I ignored. B accounts were medium size and should have taken up approximately 15% of my time, while C accounts (inevitably needier and smaller accounts) should have taken up only about 5% of my time. Reviewing my accounts, I realized I'd built a large portfolio of C accounts, which were easier to get because the competition did not want those accounts. Because I had to spend so much time on my C accounts, my time to go after A and B accounts was minimal.

To figure out what I was doing wrong, I had to work on my ability to listen, check my ego at the door, and focus on working smarter, not harder. It took me a while to start looking at the value of my time, but this brought about the biggest changes to my sales success.

Most people understand that time is money when considering the value of time in a daily business context. You earn X amount of dollars per year. That equates to Y dollars per hour. Now that I am older and have gone through major ups and downs financially, going from millennial millionaire to bankruptcy when the markets crashed in 2008 and then building it all back up again, I realize time is infinitely more valuable than money. You can always make more money. But one can never replace time. So, it's best to figure out ways to use your time efficiently for maximum return. Spending time learning from and asking questions of those in positions to teach you is never a waste.

Ask Questions of Life.

My mom is a brilliant question-asker. She's curious about other people and a natural networker. She drilled into me, from an early age, the importance of asking questions and taught me that no doesn't necessarily mean no; no just means not now. She showed me this by example, applying for business loans to thirteen banks before finally securing financing to build the first boat in her yacht charter business.

When my parents were getting divorced, they did a wonderful job of keeping things hidden from us kids as best as they could despite things being rocky. The whole ordeal went on for about two years, though it wasn't as ugly as it could have been with daily emotional outbursts and fights. My older sister Danielle was out of the house, working as a live-in babysitter with one of the neighbors, so it was mostly my brother Derek and I at home.

Still, the going wasn't easy. Talking with a divorce mediator during the divorce proceedings, I was asked, "Who do you want to live with?" I loved my mom and dad, and this was an incredibly difficult decision to make.

Though my dad and I were close, I chose to live with my mom, though it was a very tough, emotional choice. My brother went with my dad and moved about thirty-five minutes away. From that point on, we lived apart. I visited Dad on the weekends or when I could.

My mom moved up into the hills to Mill Valley, which is just north of the Golden Gate Bridge from San Francisco. It was about a thirty-five-minute scooter ride from my high school, but I was still able to attend the school I had planned to attend before the divorce, riding backroads and side streets to get there. Though my brother lived with my dad, he was able to take the bus to the same high school.

In many ways, the divorce strengthened my relationships with my parents, even though this took some maturing on my part. I appreciated the difficulty of the situation, and I learned you can pick up a lot by observing the behaviors of others, both good and bad.

I admired how Mom went about being a single mom and building her business as an entrepreneur after a divorce and so many life changes. My dad married my wonderful stepmom, Kathy, a year later, and they are happy to this day.

Despite their differences, my mom and dad were initially a good fit for the charter business they started together. Mom's outgoing nature, networking ability, and eye for design were ideally suited for some parts of the business, while Dad's mechanical knowledge and willingness to roll up his sleeves and maintain operations worked well behind the scenes. Dad had a hand in the startup of the business, helping to find and secure the first two boats.

For a time following their divorce, I thought my dad might try to get his own charter business going. He certainly had the strength when it came to mechanical operations. His get-it-done attitude was perfect for that side of the business, though interior design, fixtures, and finishing touches were not his strong suits. He is a no-nonsense type of man and did not enjoy the inevitable day-to-day staff issues, networking, or schmoozing. These components are essential to the success of many sales-oriented ventures, especially the yacht chartering, entertainment industry. In the end, it turned out the yacht charter business wasn't the right fit for him.

We all must find our own way in life. Asking questions of others and of ourselves is key to ensuring we are on the right path, especially when the path takes an unexpected turn.

My mom taught me never to be afraid to ask for help. "Even if what you're doing comes naturally to you, you'll have many questions and doubts. When I started my business, I had no idea how to read a comprehensive balance sheet, how to write a business plan, or how to handle budget projections. While growing my business, I grew myself. It was my education out of the classroom. This is the case for most entrepreneurs. Surround yourself with experts, and don't be afraid to call on them for help. Take the time to learn from these people. You must be smart enough to know when you need help."

The Magic of "Unmodeling"

Many people do the same things year after year. At work, when their performance predictably slides, they stop trying.

They go with the new flow.

While it is an individual choice to work at a certain level, I probably wouldn't want to model these people. But looking at what they *don't* do reinforces what I *must* do. For example, what are they doing to reinvent themselves, to learn new skills, and grow as an individual? How do they present themselves to co-workers and clients?

Often, when it comes to attire, people dress however they want and ignore how their clients or guests prefer to dress. Personally and professionally, first impressions count.

It is important to know your audience and clients so you can dress appropriately. Showing up for an interview in jeans and a polo shirt probably won't make the best first impression even in the techy world. I'm not saying you must wear a suit and tie as times have changed but being slightly overdressed is a much better position to take than showing up underdressed in a business situation. Remember that you can always dress down when going out in the workplace, but you will have a tough time dressing up or being presentable at the last minute. Even when visiting the techy world where jeans are prevalent, I might shed my coat, tie, and cuff links, but I still wear slacks and a dress shirt to represent myself professionally and appropriately.

Some people might say, "This is who I am. Accept me for what I say and how I look." While I love the confidence in this attitude, the reality is that most people will still judge you based upon first impressions. It's human nature. Always has been, always will be.

People who appear to be sloppy and lazy in one area might make others wonder about their work in other areas. How are their presentation, administrative, and organization skills, and overall dedication to themselves and their clients? Quite often, a person's work ethic is a mirror of their outward appearance. The way people keep their house and their car says a lot about how they maintain their life.

One of the cornerstone lessons I learned from my grandmothers and my dad is the importance of respect and manners. Hold the door open for the next person. Treat people with respect. Napkins on your lap. No elbows on the table. No swearing or foul language. Say sir and ma'am as a sign of respect. These characteristics helped me tremendously in the business world and are areas I find somewhat lacking with younger generations. If that's you, look at these things as opportunities to grow.

By developing positive etiquette and manners, you put yourself in a position to be of service and help your fellow man. In a crowded field, where everyone behaves mostly the same, your good manners will stand out. This is a good thing.

All these things remind me of an expression that sums it

all up—how you do anything is how you do everything.

Reverse-Engineer Emotions and Experiences and Chart a New Course.

To make changes for yourself and get where you want to be, be clear about your starting point. Ask yourself if your portrait of yourself is coming from your head or your heart. Don't pander to yourself. If your gut says you've got some work to do, listen.

If you spot areas you'd like to change, ask how you'll feel when you successfully change. Then ask yourself what you need to feel to bring about this change. Be specific and write things out in your notebook.

The feelings you identify, necessary to achieve fulfillment and success, will be wildly influenced by the data and references you experience through your five senses. Your perspective, self-talk, faith, and body structure will serve as the necessary building blocks to set up the state needed to manage ultimate growth.

Now, ask what must happen for you to feel the way you want to feel more often. What changes must you make? What does not committing to this change now cost you? Who else will benefit from this change? Why is it necessary you stay 100% committed and change now?

This self-reflection can be as simple as noting you are happiest when you walk your dog or go for a jog, then committing to making it happen every day for fifteen minutes. If you're reaching for something that seems out of reach, look around and find someone doing what you want to do, and approach them for advice.

Many of us make it ridiculously hard to achieve happiness because we have so many rules for what needs to happen first. For example, a person might have rules that say they are happy when they can go on vacation. We all love a nice vacation, but how often does one get to go on vacation? Do the vacations-equal-happiness people choose to be miserable at other times? Yikes!

Some people say they will feel fulfilled when they have a Porsche in the driveway, a beautiful partner, two kids, a membership at the country club, or millions in the bank. So many things need to happen for them to be happy that they're miserable.

Choose instead to feel happy simply because you choose to every day. Live in a state of gratitude. Allow yourself to feel overwhelmed that you have a beating heart and can see the world, speak to others, walk, talk, hear, and make the determination of what anything means to you while pursuing all your dreams. Realize how much of this is an impossibility for others.

It is our decision to live in a beautiful emotional state, so don't wait any longer. Choose now.

What Personality Are You Bringing to the Party?

Most of us can tap into different mindsets or personalities to achieve a goal, though some people might not be aware of this powerful tool or how to use it. Others are highly proficient at this and do it subconsciously.

Depending on the goal and situation, one can dramatically improve the chances of meeting their outcomes simply by stepping into a different persona. For example, if a naturally shy person is asked to give a TED talk or a presentation to a large group, they must tap into their tool chest of personalities for one that will get the job done.

To do this, take a deep breath and stand the way you stand when you know this is your moment. Feel the energy flow from the crowd as you own the space where you will share your experience and supply value for all the amazing people watching you. Hear their applause in support of you. Own the moment and be grateful for the opportunity! Close your eyes and ask, with deeply held emotion, focus, and a belief in yourself, which personality will get you to the winning side. You may choose to name this personality, so you can reference it whenever you need it in the future. For example, a few personality names I reference in different situations are Fearless D, Empathetic D, Inspirational D, and Relentless D.

Visualize how you will stand, walk, breathe, and talk as you present a tremendous speech to a welcoming audience. I encourage you to visualize in advance the feelings of accomplishment your impactful and inspirational speech will have, the impact on many souls, and the feelings of accomplishment and pride that will come to you after walking offstage to a rousing ovation. Take a minute to imagine the other positive feelings you might feel. Let your imagination go and really visualize all that you see, hear, and feel during the speech and just after walking away to the many warm and thankful smiles.

Next, you will step into that personality. Our emotional state is vital as, without the best one for the job, we go nowhere. Thus, we need to make sure our emotional state is congruent with what we want to achieve. This could mean making a rapid change in our body structure or physiology, which helps us get in the desired state instantly. I think of this as a power move.

In short, a power move is a unique physical motion that engages your body by anchoring positive emotions, feelings, and focus. By anchoring this movement at the peak of experiencing these resources, we can effectively trigger and recall these characteristics to create a powerful identity that we can use anytime we want.

There is not any right or wrong move. My mentor, Tony Robbins, has a power move that allows him to go from a disempowered state to an empowered state instantly. Tony uses various power moves like strongly hitting his chest simultaneously with both hands. Another is snapping his right arm down as if a sudden bolt of energy surges through his body and arm.

Many athletes do their own versions of power moves to get themselves into the right emotional states. The multi-gold medalist and world-record sprint champion, Usain Bolt, extends his left arm, pointing diagonally toward the sky, and presses his right hand close to his body, pointing in the same direction, symbolizing a lightning bolt.

Experiment with different moves until one feels right for you. Then, put your body and personality into your new moves, even if you feel as if you are acting. Unless you're an actor, you're not acting! You're just tapping into a part of you that might usually not be at the forefront of your behavior.

If you have a tough time embodying this powerful version of yourself, think about someone you admire who would be able to manage the obstacle you wish to overcome. Then, ask how they'd do it. Ask yourself what this person embodies that gives you confidence they would reach the desired outcome. For example, are they powerful, courageous, resilient, or do they have some other attribute? Write down at least three strengths your chosen model personality has. Then, close your eyes and step into the shoes of your role model, feeling fully associated with each attribute they have. See what you saw, hear what you heard, and feel what you felt as your powerful and chosen personality characteristics helped you in handling the situation yourself. The more detail the better as you visualize the various emotional states you feel. Do this enough, and you'll find it gets much easier to model and pick the personalities that will help you get through to the other desired side of any challenge.

Don't-Do Lists

While examining the bad habits of others can help us see what we need to work on for ourselves, I don't recommend spending too much time focusing on what not to do. Some people keep a list of bad habits they want to be reminded not to do. While I appreciate this idea, I find focusing on my goals and what I will do to accomplish them is more productive.

It's always best to frame things in a positive light and direct your energy toward a positive outcome. In doing so, you'll accomplish the items on your to-do list and avoid the need to divert energy into what you shouldn't be doing. If you know you shouldn't be doing something because it's holding you back in any area of your life, then don't do it. Simple.

Learning, Modeling, and Independence

When I was a kid, my parents bought fixer-upper boats that we cruised from Ft. Lauderdale through the Panama Canal, up the coasts of Central America and Mexico, and along the west coast of the United States, beginning my love affair with travel and adventure.

Driving my scooter through the back roads on the way to school gave me a sense of adventure, freedom, and a taste for being outdoors. When I was sixteen, I went to Spain as an exchange student in Barcelona and the island of Mallorca. I lived near the beach with a group of Spanish friends, all experiencing life away from home too.

After my sophomore year in college, I planned to return to Europe with a friend of mine and tour around during the summer. When he couldn't make it at the last minute, I decided to go by myself and pursue this once-in-a-lifetime adventure. I modeled my parent's behavior and sense of adventure without thinking of it that way.

I flew from San Francisco to Amsterdam with nothing but a duffle bag over my shoulder and a *Let's Go* book of Europe. I spent $565 on my plane ticket, $365 on a one-month unlimited Eurail pass, and I had $1,100 cash for the entire fifty days I planned to stay. I didn't have a planned itinerary, but I wanted to visit as many countries and cultures as possible. I never worried and had the time of my life.

What I did learn was how creative you can become on a shoestring budget and, more importantly, how your mindset and attitude dictate the success of your experiences. I strategically spent some nights on overnight trains and then stayed in hostels, slept outdoors with other backpackers, and ate creatively. My total all-in budget for everything was a whopping $22 a day, but I made it work.

My European trip was an unforgettable adventure and a priceless experience. Not worrying about money, I made some of the most magical memories of my life. My epic journey of discovery took me to Amsterdam, Belgium, Paris, southern France, and Spain in the first ten days. I traveled by bus and hitchhiked. I had friends in Spain from my previous high school adventure, so I had a place to stay while I was there. After my time in Spain, I traveled east across the French Riviera, to Italy, down to Greece and its islands, back to the mainland, and on to Austria, Switzerland, and Germany. Ultimately, I traveled back to Amsterdam, all within my pre-planned schedule, using my rail pass.

I know now that I was successful at completing this epic journey because of my independence, determination, vision, strategic-planning abilities, and creative, positive, carefree attitude and mindset. These ingredients made all the difference and are things anyone can nurture within themselves.

I've always been independent. One of the reasons I'm comfortable going off on adventures and doing my own thing stems from something I heard countless times growing up—"Eagles don't flock," my father always told me. In other words, you don't have to follow the flock all the time.

It's okay to be different, unusual, and even a little weird. In fact, there is tremendous freedom in blazing your own trail, provided you can get past the naysayers and all the static coming from the fearful herd.

My parents instilled in me a level of confidence and a you-can-do-it attitude. I can still hear my parents and Papa (my granddad) telling me, "You can do this. Don't let anyone tell you that you can't do something." Their philosophy, when facing a challenge or setback, was to always get back on the horse and keep riding.

Don't be afraid to take the road less traveled because when you do, you're never failing. What other people think of you is their problem and doesn't have to become your reality.

My dad's a tinkerer when it comes to all things mechanical. He loves taking stuff apart, breaking it down, and figuring out how it works. On his property, right now, he has various Model A cars that have been restored. He and Kathy take considerable pride in their cars. He's not afraid to do some repairs and restoration himself and work his way into areas where he has never gone before. There is a level of cool confidence about him that comes from figuring things out on his own that I respect and admire.

My parents also taught me to take pride in being the underdog. "The greater the adversity, the greater the hero," Mom said. As the underdog, she made waves in the male-dominated yacht chartering business, despite the naysayers.

If someone does not believe in you, go to work with vigor and make your dreams a reality. The doubters will go away as your success builds, and you will find your tribe and build your team.

My dad and mom started their business together, buying their first fixer-upper boat when they were still married. Dad had excellent mechanical skills and could fix just about anything on the boat. Mom was the networker, cook, and entertainer. They complemented one another and made an effective team.

When they divorced, my mom kept the rights to the startup business. At first, she was perceived as a little Latino lady going after a seemingly impossible dream. Still, she steadily grew the business and went on to be named woman entrepreneur of the year in San Francisco. Getting financing to build a reputable yacht was difficult, but she was like a dog with a bone she wouldn't let go of, and she prevailed.

From her, I learned the value of persistence, tenacity, relentlessness, and believing in yourself with all your heart. Watching Mom reinforced my understanding of the power of a positive mindset, displaying a strong will, wearing a smile, and being kind and generous to people around you. It was a combination of these factors that led Mom down the road to success.

Though the period of my life when my parents were separating was difficult, I recognized the value of their individual strengths. I began adopting positive aspects of character from each of them. I learned that being analytical, thinking, forming opinions, and then sticking to your guns is essential in business and in life.

Any situation that involves working on a team or

standing up for yourself requires a certain level of confidence and independence. People skills and the ability to get involved in social or networking circles are essential too. For some people, this comes naturally. For others, it's gut-wrenching work. It's not surprising that some people would rather work eight hours of hard labor in the blazing sun than put on a jacket and go to a meeting or sales call.

I'm grateful to have been exposed to the distinct characteristics of my parents, as these qualities helped me build a successful business and family and have contributed to my well-rounded existence.

Take the time to examine your own influences for the positives they give you. Seek out new relationships to fill in areas where you might feel lacking. Realize you can always build on what you have by growing something that will serve you better.

Taking the Sure Path and Following Proven Principles

There are times when we may be tempted to go for the glory road or make a move that only serves our vanity instead of taking the sure path to success. These choices are always worth pausing over. Examine your motivations before deciding the best course of action.

When I was in college, I took part in a pick-up basketball

game. It wasn't a league game or of any major importance. Toward the end of the game, we were tied 10-10. The team that made the next basket would win.

The other team had the ball and was threatening to win when I stole the ball away and charged down the court, two steps ahead of the other team's players. I could have easily made the layup and won the game. But I was a smaller player who'd always wanted to dunk the ball in a game for glory's sake, something I had only achieved five times before in practice. Even though I was short, I was still a good jumper because of my long-jump experience. So, making a snap decision to go for the dunk, I leaped high into the air with the ball in my left hand. It slipped out of my grip at the apex of my jump. My wrist slapped off the rim, sending the ball ricocheting to the other team.

It happened so fast; I had blown the dunk! The other team snatched the ball, went down the court quickly, and scored the winning point. The disappointment in my teammate's faces was heartbreaking. They could not believe I hadn't made the fundamental play to clinch the game.

The lesson I learned that day was to consider the landscape of the events you're working with. If I had paused, I might have realized this was a team event and remembered other people were counting on me as a member of the team to focus on our goal, winning the game.

Granted, this wasn't a championship league game, and there were only a handful of people in the stands. When it was over, who won didn't matter all that much. Yet, to this day, this experience lives in my memory despite the hundreds of pickup basketball games I have played since. I'll never forget my teammates asking me what I was thinking and why I hadn't gone for the sure thing.

Sometimes, in life, it pays to go for the sure thing, especially when others are involved and counting on you. Serve the greater good instead of feeding your own ego. Follow the examples of champions and become one yourself.

Keys:

Model authentic and genuine people.

There are a lot of posers and fake people out there, primarily focused on promoting their own agenda. When you are modeling people within a specific industry, their results will speak for themselves, are readily available, and can be verified.

A good place to start with people you don't know, who may present themselves as a leader backed by a credible success story, is to do some legwork on social media to get a clear picture of who you are dealing with. If their profile is all about them and the fantastic things they are doing and places they are going, be aware that you may be viewing only their highlight reel. Many people post these highlights to validate and elevate themselves above others in a self-serving manner. Keep digging until you are sure you're in the hands of an authentic authority.

Check your peer group.

Take a close look at the people who surround you. Are they like-minded and supportive of your efforts? Pay attention to the five people closest to you. Some of them may be your family members. You may love your family, but they could exert tremendous influence over you, not always in a positive way.

It's okay to check out and establish boundaries. Don't be afraid to limit your time with anyone who holds you back or brings you down. I have been fortunate to have a very loving extended family and good friends; however, not everyone is as fortunate as I have been in this area. Remember, you can love your family and still choose your peer group.

Be consistent and stay the course.

It's common practice to start down a new path, then drop off within a short time. Every new endeavor will run into roadblocks and challenges. Being persistent will keep you moving forward.

Persistence is a major part of achieving success in any area, so much so that I've devoted a whole chapter to it later in this book.

The best way to apply persistence is by developing consistent work habits and an ability to break tasks into bite-sized pieces. Daily, regular efforts always move you toward your goals. When modeling someone you believe is persistent and has a persistent mindset, focus on what they do every day, every week, and every month. It's these consistent actions you want to adopt and apply to your life.

Focus.

People who get superior results focus on what they are doing while they are doing it. They step back periodically to monitor their results. They ask, "What's working? What isn't working?" This allows them to adjust their game plan and consistently try new approaches when necessary.

Establish rapport.

Forming a positive connection with people you wish to model helps in two ways. First, it reinforces that you are serious about what you are doing and respect the time your mentor spends helping you. Second, unless you have a good rapport with people you ask for help it is difficult to accept feedback and critique without getting defensive or feeling let down.

If I were to model Debbi Fields, founder of Mrs. Fields, one of the leading cookie makers in the United States, I would make sure to follow through with the information she shared with me and communicate my gratitude for the time she spent helping me. To reinforce our rapport together, I would show her what I accomplished based upon her insights and make sure to offer to reciprocate any way I could to help serve her in return.

 **Tools:**

It is important to model the most successful, well-rounded people, wealthy in the areas of life you want to have. Before modeling and replicating your best role models, do your homework and figure out the following:

1. Understand their why in life. Ask why they are doing what they are doing.

2. Explore the driving force behind their success. What do they attribute their success to? Be clear as to what success means to them. Is it just monetary or emotional fulfillment?

3. Finding out what inspires your mentor will tell you if similar motivations exist for you. Why would you want to replicate someone who doesn't exemplify who you are at your core?

   Living a life that is not congruent with who you really are is a recipe for emptiness and no emotional fulfillment. You might become wealthy by modeling someone rich, who is not in alignment with you deep down, but this will never lead you to an empowering place. Success without fulfillment is failure.

For inspiration, check out these opportunities to learn from masterminds while building relationships.

- Your Best Life – Offers selective, dynamic, one-on-one, group, and company coaching.

- Tony Robbins – Tony is the master of life-transformational work and offers many courses. This is where I got my start along with many of my colleagues and is the basis of a lot of my work and success. I continue to participate in this wonderful organization today, enjoying the constant learning, fulfilling long-term relationships, and the opportunity to give back at a high level.

- GOBUNDANCE – This is a tribe of healthy, wealthy, generous men who choose to lead epic lives. I am an originating member, and some great friendships of mine have evolved from this group.

- Rock Thomas – Rock's organization helps people become whole life millionaires not just financially but also in all areas of their life—health, wealth, and relationships.

CHAPTER 3

Purpose

Efforts and courage are not enough without purpose and direction.

John F. Kennedy

Your purpose, simply put, is what you want to contribute to the world and is a direct reflection of your identity. But purpose without well-thought-out reasons, or your why, won't get you far. Your whys must be strong because they are what will get you motivated every day to work hard toward your goals.

Your purpose and your mission reflect why you believe

you are here. I recommend everyone develop a mission statement that reflects their individual and unique purpose in life.

What Do You Want, and Why Do You Want it?

The best purpose statements strike to the heart of who you are. They challenge you to be true to yourself. For instance, "I share to inspire others and appreciate my God-given gifts," helps me make choices that align with my best self and highest purpose. This purpose and the why behind it is what influences everything I do.

Loving, giving, and inspiring are the central components of many identity statements and purposes in life. I'm a big love bug and kind of cheesy at times. I dig romantic movies and am not afraid to admit it. *The Notebook*, *Jerry Maguire*, *Notting Hill*, and *A Star is Born* are movies that I have no problem seeing over and over again. These types of movies often make me teary-eyed, and that's okay. I embrace this part of my identity, in large part, because I've spent so much time dialing into my ultimate purpose and embracing my loving nature. Sharing movies is just one way to express love and inspire others.

Inspiring others to go to higher heights is one of life's great joys. When I'm helping others to push themselves farther, I receive joy and love in return. This means I am not only serving others, but I'm also serving myself on the back end as well. This doesn't take away from the genuine nature of my service to others, as I never come from a selfish place. Supporting others comes naturally because I have a lot of love in my heart to share.

Offering a helping hand to other people is a win-win all around. The best purposes and whys fit this model. They fill you with passion, and have a strong why behind them, and give something to those around you.

My clarity of purpose helps me feel loved every day. When I open my eyes in the morning, it's as if the heavens are looking down on me and giving me another day to share with the world. Love is always felt because my heart is beating! When people smile at me, I feel a sense of connection and love. This makes me want to do the same in return; however, I try and make it a point to be the instigator and smile first. I don't want my happiness to be contingent on someone else smiling at me or something out of my control.

I make it amazingly easy to feel good. My clarity allows me to do this, and because my purpose is clear and my "rules" are so easy to achieve, I'm able to express love for people in many ways. Though the ways I express my love for others might seem like little things, this sharing of my caring self could make someone else's day or help positively shift their focus. You never know what's going on with people or the impact you might have on their lives.

Life's Events Can Shape Purpose

A friend of mine I have known since high school, Bryan Boches, recently commented on my Facebook post about a speedy downhill ski run I'd laid down in perfect early morning conditions. "You must have nine lives because you keep bouncing back from the edge and pushing the limits!" he said.

He reminded me of a mountain biking trip we took together in high school, where I should have died but came away unscathed. A pack of us were moving quickly along the edge of a steep hillside when my front tire slipped off the single-track trail near a deep ravine that was about ten feet across and thirty feet deep. I hit both brakes with maximum force, but the front brake had too much tension combined with the downhill momentum. My back tire somersaulted over the handlebars toward the ravine. My bike caught up in a bush growing at the base of a large tree on the edge of the ravine trail. I desperately tried to grab the tree in midair; however, I could not reach it, and I fell uncontrollably backward to the sloped ground. My feet hit approximately ten feet below the trail, and my momentum carried me in a slow backflip to the bottom of the canyon twenty-five feet below. I thought my short life was ending as my body quickly shot downward. Miraculously, I landed on my feet between two big boulders, completely stunned. No broken bones and not a scratch on me. I hadn't even tweaked my back! It took a second to absorb what had happened, but when it hit me that I was all right, I let out a loud, warrior scream of relief. It was a miracle! My friends expressed complete disbelief, unable to believe what they had just seen. But I realized my time had not come yet.

My friends and I laugh about my death-defying fall to this day, but I also took to heart the realization that I must have a higher purpose in this life and that my work, loving and helping others, is not finished.

Visualizing Your Best Life

Many people don't realize what their best life could be. They might not spend much time thinking about it and are simply going through the motions every day, floating along on whatever tide life brings. This is a sad state to live in. It can suck you so dry you can't even imagine a better life. I have been there myself. Your purpose gets lost.

When you're living your best life, you are likely living

your true purpose as well. So, let's keep getting in touch with and refining your purpose, whether you have one or need to find one.

One of the best ways to discover your purpose is to figure out what your best life looks like. To do that, you must be specific and highly detailed. Start by writing in your notebook all the thoughts and images of everything you want in your life. Don't be shy. It is time to let your imagination be free of any preconceived borders. Do not try and keep your thoughts in your head and take the easy way out by not putting them on paper.

Once your visions gain more clarity, cut out images from magazines that represent the life of your dreams, and create a vision board. These images can come from the internet or magazines and postcards. Your vision board can be a physical place where you pin your pictures, or it can be online. Some people make their list of words or pictures the screensaver on their computer or phone. For example, among many images, my personal vision board from two years ago had a picture of a baby, pictures of exotic places I wanted the family to see, financial and investment numbers, and pictures of myself, speaking for and inspiring a large audience. I was blessed to achieve each one.

The more you see your vision, the more you will absorb it, and the stronger your purpose will become.

Pinterest is a popular website for storing vision boards. Look for themes and patterns in your words and pictures. When the same words and pictures keep coming up, you're on the right track. Seeing your best life in pictures and reading about it in your notebook will help you visualize and manifest it. This is key to making it a reality.

As you write in your notebook, ask yourself, "What are my top strengths?" Also, "What do I truly enjoy doing?" We cannot manifest anything that we enjoy doing in our life without identifying it first.

It might take some soul searching to identify your core values, but aligning your strengths (normally what you enjoy doing) with your values makes your purpose much clearer.

This process is all about you. Your purpose in life is not dependent upon other people. This is important because it's easy to become discouraged when other people don't respond to your work or criticize you because they don't see things the same way you do.

Stay your course. It is up to you to be the best possible version of yourself. Live with no masks. Be your awesome, authentic self!

When you follow your heart and genuinely do your best, you can accomplish almost anything, inspiring people, changing lives, and making a positive difference.

Reasons, Motivation, and Fuel

Setting and reaching our goals requires clarity about our reasons, motivation, and fuel. All three components are related to your why, the most critical area of goal setting because it's a direct pipeline to your heart and soul. If your reasons for doing something are not strong enough, the mechanics of the goal-setting process are not going to happen.

We're all guilty of going through the motions, feeling as if we're making progress because of the swirl of activity surrounding us. At times, knocking things off my to-do list left and right, too busy to come up for air, I felt I was making strides in life. But I was just busy with things that didn't increase my sense of inner-peace or create a sense of emotional fulfillment.

Be careful not to equate activity to accomplishment. In this context, I mean the accomplishment of a deeper level of fulfillment connected to your true purpose.

Focus on clarity by examining your reasons for the things you spend time on and reinforcing your why. When someone asks you about your business or purpose, words should flow naturally from you, without hesitation, like a thirty-second elevator speech.

Motivation and energy (fuel) are natural by-products of

clearly knowing why you want what you want and reinforcing it regularly.

Finding Your Calling When Your Path Wanders

I've found my true calling in life by inspiring and serving others. I have grown my businesses built on this philosophy. By focusing on and serving my customers and contributing to the company, I've created flexibility and freedom in my life. As a result, I feel a greater sense of peace, joy, and love in my heart. This makes me happy, which goes right back to my love of helping and serving everyone around me. Everyone wins!

This calling also led me to dedicate myself to education and training, helping others to succeed. My primary motivation for writing this book comes directly from this dedication too and fits with the clear purpose for my life. Whenever I share what I've learned, whether through my experiences or as a student of the school of hard knocks, it brings me extraordinary joy. Helping reduce the learning curve for others fits squarely with my overall purpose.

As an advocate for continued education and lifelong learning, I routinely attend various personal development workshops and seminars and regularly contribute my services, giving to others, and keeping myself on track by living my purpose.

Living your purpose is easy to do when your purpose and your why are clear. When you spend time dialing them in for yourself, you're easily able to identify pursuits and actions that support your best life and spend a lot less time spinning your wheels and getting nowhere.

Sometimes, it helps to look at your past. Search for patterns to help you uncover your true purpose or passion, especially when the path to where you are today has taken some turns and hasn't been a steady line.

I remember repeatedly riding my bike past the house of the wealthiest man in my community when I was about ten years old, wondering who lived there and how they had accumulated their wealth. I was an innocent and curious ten-year-old stalker on a bike as my curiosity ran to why this person owned half a block on the water in Marin County, just outside of San Francisco. The house was owned by an heir to the Anheuser-Busch family, but I had no idea what that meant.

I decided there might be an opportunity to provide some form of service for such a grand place and decided to give it a shot. My effort paid off when the maintenance manager hired me to help in the garden. Though I was more of a glorified weed puller, I learned a valuable lesson. Regardless of the task at hand, I took pleasure in doing the best job possible. This experience also helped me develop a strong work ethic at an early age.

In high school, I worked on one of the boats in my mom's company. I washed dishes, waited tables, worked as a deckhand, and did anything else that was needed. This work continued into my college years when I would come home for the summer from UC Santa Barbara. Working hard all along, I was given more responsibilities, acting as a host, busboy, and bartender for events. Even though these roles didn't make me financially free by any means, I learned about managing responsibilities and developed the practice of being flexible. I also learned the value of multi-tasking and team collaboration, honing my desire to serve others and bring them happiness. This was a priceless education, cementing my solid work ethic and making it a part of my nature. More opportunities seemed to magically appear in my life.

At UC Santa Barbara, I became an English major to improve my communication skills. Originally, I planned to major in business, but at the time, UCSB only offered business economics as a major. I had a tough time with all the classic literature and hated the material. At the advice of some folks in my inner circle, I decided to focus on the bigger picture and use this experience to broaden my communication and relationship-building skills. There are thousands of business majors seeking work after college, but not all of them can speak, present, write, and connect with people on a deeper level. These skills will always be in demand in the business world, especially in sales. Even then, I was developing my ability to shift my attitude toward success and ensure that no matter what I had to do, I was working toward a deeper goal.

After college, I wasn't sure what I wanted to do, but I knew I loved to ski, so I took some time off to ski various resorts in Utah before finding a job at the awesome resort of Snowbird. I performed the wonderful task of washing dishes at The Cliff Lodge, five days a week at 5:00 PM, so I could ski the chutes and moguls with other ski bum friends every day and do what I truly wanted to do. Perhaps it wasn't the ideal job for a person who'd just earned their college degree, but I had the time of my life! I rented a tiny room in the town of Sandy at the base of Cottonwood Canyon and often hitchhiked up and down to Snowbird to wash dishes six hours a night. My beat-up car would not make it safely up and down the canyon on snow days, so it was better to hitchhike. People often offered rides back in the day.

Once my time as a ski bum ran its course, I still wasn't sure of my calling in life. I decided to go back to Barcelona for the 1992 summer Olympic games. This was a magical summer as I met a US athlete and his family who took in my grandfather and me. We were blessed to see many complimentary sporting events as the tickets were given to us daily by AT&T, who sponsored all the families and athletes. Meeting many of the athletes was inspiring. I saw the dedication it took to represent the United States, and seeing the original, famous USA basketball dream team play twice was amazing!

After Spain, I went back to the Bay area. I worked for my mom and waited tables at a few restaurants in San Francisco. For a brief stint, I lived in Los Angeles while trying to make it as an actor and model. In hindsight, these experiences helped reinforce my skills as a waiter and served as a clear reminder of the importance of knowing my why and purpose and helped steer me clear of doing things that didn't serve me.

The final straw came when I was on a modeling shoot, with my clothes off down to my skivvies, and the photographer wanted me to bare it all, which I wasn't willing to do. He reminded me that he knew a lot of people in the business and challenged me, asking, "How bad do you want to propel your career? I know a lot of contacts and casting directors whom I can refer you to tomorrow."

I guess I didn't want it that bad because I immediately decided to return to San Francisco and regroup.

Things happen for a reason, and shortly after my return to the Bay area, I landed a job in the medical distribution field with Physician Sales and Service (later bought out by McKesson).

At the time, Physicians Sales and Service (PSS) was in Costa Mesa, California. I worked my tail off, putting in seventy hours a week in their warehouse doing everything possible—from scrubbing toilets, vacuuming, picking and packing, to delivering orders for the account managers—all while earning $1,500 a month.

I was determined not to let the work or hours break me as I knew successful salespeople in this field. Though the hours were hellish, I kept my eye on the long-term goal and outworked the other people who were hired around the same time, making it through the three-month break-in period when most people quit.

After the term was completed, I was blessed to get a sales territory in the San Francisco Bay area. It was an incredibly challenging area. I was the third account manager in two years because PSS had struggled to gain market share, which was dominated by the large company, McKesson, which had a very long-standing reputation for excellence. Their tenured representatives enjoyed long-term relationships with most of the accounts in the area. Nevertheless, I hustled and persevered, worked even more hours a month, and called on every McKesson account, trying to build my portfolio of business.

Three and a half years later, McKesson took notice. They wanted me to join them. My scrappy style of getting things done had put me on their radar!

Brad Jacob, a competitor who was the top sales executive at McKesson and is now a good friend and mentor of mine, called me unexpectedly. I was humbled because Brad was playing in an ocean, and I was in a different league—the little man's league.

McKesson wanted to hire me but didn't offer me anything that inspired me to make the leap and switch companies, so I held out. A few months later, they brought me back in and still would not budge, so neither did I.

Thankfully, three months later, at a conference, Brad called me and said the President of McKesson, Rick Frey, wanted to speak to Brad and me at his hotel. Nervous as heck, I went, and within no time, Rick gave me the signing bonus and additional money I felt I was worth. My career was taking off!

A solid work ethic, coupled with focus and an emerging sense of purpose, led me in the right direction and to where I am today. My experiences all gave me opportunities to learn. At McKesson, I was able to model the habits of the best of the best.

Brad is widely known as the most successful sales account executive ever in the history of medical distribution sales, so I was learning from the best. Kevin O'Regan, my McKesson sales manager, brought me under his wing and gave me the freedom to go get business wherever I could, which was a blessing. Immediately, I started to grow and grow.

Pretty amazing to look back at the rambling path I took to get there and see how each experience brought me there.

When you look at your life, know that things happen for a reason, and life unfolds as it is meant to unfold. Sometimes, a meandering path shows you the way if you are patient and take the time to get to know yourself along the way.

My experiences working for my mom's yacht charter business helped shape the person I am today. I am grateful for them, even though working in that business wasn't what I ultimately wanted to do. Though Mom would have liked me to take on more responsibilities and leadership roles until I ultimately took over the operations of the business, I knew, from trial and experience, that I wanted something different for my life. My desire to establish my own identity and create my own success was strong.

My mom had become well-known in the industry, and around town, as Marti McMahon, the yacht lady. Many people connected me to her, and I was often introduced as Marti's son. On the one hand, you might view this as a positive thing with the potential to open many doors. For me, it cast a shadow that went against my nature. Sorry, Mom. I love you even though it was necessary for me to carve out my own identity.

I know many people who grew up working in their parent's business and went on to take over the next generation, growing the company and building it in new and different directions. That's wonderful when it fits your passion and skills, as well as your purpose in life. But the food and beverage industry, hosting parties and celebrations on yachts, just wasn't for me. I knew I wanted to serve people in a different capacity, though it took a while to figure out exactly what that was.

It wasn't until I attended my first Tony Robbins seminar in my early thirties that I began to see the opportunities to help people in the personal development space that felt in line with my true purpose.

Fulfillment Doesn't Always Equal Money

I was a slow learner! It wasn't until I was about forty years old that I began to change my mindset when it came to money, fulfillment, and success. I had been involved in a long-term, on-again, off-again relationship with a woman who lived in Europe. She was a beautiful soul, and I enjoyed the years we spent traveling around the world. But it became challenging due to our differences. I was a big believer in investing in yourself and in the personal development space, while she believed one should figure life out for themselves. She came from a background of five-star travel and had extravagant tastes. Having been a successful print and runway model for ten years in Europe, she was used to a very high level of living. During the period we dated, I was wealthy on paper, but from a cash flow position, I struggled to keep up with her expectations.

The stress of keeping up appearances and pursuing the almighty dollar began to take a toll on my health. Over time, I realized I hadn't been genuine and real with her or myself from the start, so I was the source of my own frustrations, trying to be someone I was not. I was guilty of living with the mask seen so prevalently in society today.

I got a lot of emotional fulfillment from simpler things in life, but I wasn't living my life that way.

Looking at my history of carefree travels on a shoestring budget, I see now that this extravagant lifestyle didn't fit me. Some of the happiest times in my life were about the journey and the adventure, not ratings, luxury, fitting an image, or the high cost of admission.

This realization helped me when, in 2008, the financial markets and the real estate market took a nosedive. I found myself in real trouble. This was when I began to realize the value of emotional fulfillment over financial success.

In hindsight, I see I'd focused on pleasing my girlfriend. Although I loved her and did my best to fulfill her, I wasn't fulfilled myself. To love someone, you need to be happy with who you are, fulfilling your own needs, and following your true path in life. It is especially important to love oneself 100%, unconditionally, before one is ready for a loving, tender relationship with the right person. By wearing a mask and focusing solely on my girlfriend, I hadn't been genuine.

To get to where I wanted to be in life and as a person, I had to change my focus and my priorities. I needed to get real and be true to myself about who I was, what made me happy, and what I needed to do.

My life experiences taught me that material wealth is nice, and in some ways, it's important, but it pales in comparison to emotional wealth and well-being.

Our life journeys and lessons are as unique as we are. What have you learned about yourself so far?

How Do You Define Success?

Success means different things to different people. I know people who sometimes struggle, wanting a life of service or peace, without all the material things society indicates as successful like huge houses, impressive job titles, or fancy cars. They are genuinely happy with less material things, striving instead for a greater bounty of inner wealth. Others will never be happy unless they have all the things money can buy.

Both views are okay. All these people can be successful. The trick is to find out what success means to you and build your life around achieving it.

I define success as being able to look at yourself at the end of the day and know you have put 100% into seeking whatever is important to you in life. This will determine the measurement of your success.

Success should not be judged by income alone. A better yardstick to measure success is emotional fulfillment.

Only you can determine what success means to you. Only you can determine what events and results mean. If you have everything you need in a material sense (food, clothing, and shelter) and you are emotionally fulfilled and living the life of your own choosing, you are successful. What you have could easily serve as a guide to others and inspire them to look inside themselves for fulfillment.

Dealing with Failing

As you take stock of your life, you might find yourself spending more time on the events you perceive as failures. If this happens to you, remember that there are no failures in life. Mistakes and so-called failures are learning opportunities. I look at them as chances to figure things out about myself as I work my way through life. The more in touch with myself I become, the greater my sense of confidence and my attitude of personal responsibility grows.

If you're not happy with the program that's currently playing in your life, then change the station.

If you work for yourself and are constantly running late or forgetting appointments, ask yourself, "Who is the jerk setting my schedule?" You have the power to make changes and corrections at any point. You are in charge, and you define your purpose.

Learn from your experiences and focus on tweaks that will bring you closer to your ideal version of yourself.

Keys:

Live freely without a mask.

Many people go to work and put on a mask to help them do business or to create a certain persona. Sometimes, this is necessary to take care of priorities, have a job, and support your family. The trouble is when you don't know how to take the mask off when you get home or when the roles you play start to feel like who you are.

Much of this mask-wearing behavior starts at an early age when we are trying to fit in and gain acceptance with other kids.

It's important to teach young children to honor who they are because the world needs distinctive people who deliver the gifts they were given in a positive way. In a business environment, uniqueness makes you more valuable and marketable because you will be more creative and think differently from everyone else.

Standing out and above the crowd is a desirable quality that commands respect. Never forget this if you find yourself tempted to change yourself to fit in.

Love yourself and embrace the brilliance and splendor of you.

Embracing your individuality allows you to develop the ability to love yourself, putting yourself in a better position to love and embrace others. Your life is more meaningful and fulfilling when you love yourself. The world becomes a better place with you in it. It's a ripple effect of goodness.

Understand and apply the fab four.

Your physiology, self-talk, focus, and faith will help you solidify your identity while keeping you in alignment with your ultimate destination. When one's physiology is in a strong state and is combined with focus and clear language, their faith will allow them to reach their purpose.

Faith is the ability to be resilient and have clarity until the end goal is reached. Our purpose and end goals will be tested over and over, but with faith, and by using the fab four, the sky is the limit.

All four of these areas work together and influence the others. When your physiology is suffering, you're physically worn down and likely to talk to yourself in less than empowering ways. Your focus on your goals and purpose in life will be hazy and unclear. Conversely, when you feel strong and live strong physically, the words you think and say tend to be more positive and lead to a clearer focus on your goals. This clear focus leads to action and forward motion, which leads to more positive self-talk and greater focus. Faith soon follows. It's like a magical Ferris wheel of goodness that never stops.

 **Tools:**

Change your emotional state instantly by using the power of the fab four. Have you ever noticed that when someone is in a sad, disempowered state, their body always reflects this state of being? For example, they stand with shoulders slumped, eyes down, not smiling, and their chest caved in. On the flip side, if one rapidly changes their body and stands straight, puffs their chest out, puts on a big ambitious smile, and a confident walk, they instantly feel better.

The next time you feel down or defeated or catch yourself in a less-than-desirable state of being, change your body stance, your focus, and your words to immediately pull yourself back into a good space.

Watch your self-talk. Master your language, and you master your life! If you allow crappy language to saturate your mind and thoughts, then success will be a battle. We all have chatter that forms a buzz in the background of our minds. Much of it can be negative unless we train ourselves to become conscious of it and work to make our mind's babble work for us, not inhibit us.

Strive for positive language and questions, not

debilitating talk between your ears. One of the best books about how to make this happen consistently is *What to Say When You Talk to Yourself* by Shad Helmstetter, Ph.D. Pick up a copy and take your self-talk to the next level.

Perspective (Focus). Where focus goes, energy flows. If you want to reach any result or goal, you must have focus. The more focus you have, the quicker you will get to your desired destination.

The most monetarily and emotionally successful people I know are extremely disciplined in their focus. They do not waste time on worry. If you do not want something, why waste time focusing on it?

A wonderful tool to build your focus skills is meditation. There are many videos available on YouTube to guide you to the right practice for you.

Chapter 4

Goals

If you have built castles in the air, your work need not be lost; that is where they should be. Now put the foundations under them.

Henry David Thoreau

It was as a sunny, powder day. I peered at the Bear Valley Kuma cliff while going up the chair lift with my longtime ski buddy, Derek Carlson. We awoke to almost two feet of snow and excitedly hurried from our cabin to the resort to ensure we had first tracks.

Many years and countless chairlifts had come and gone,

but this forty-five-foot cliff had mesmerized us both. We were determined to finally cross this feat off our bucket lists.

This was the day we had been waiting for. Mother nature had been good to us, and the dry snow was ready to be taken.

As I got off the lift, my heart raced. My skis sunk slowly into the powdery snow. I buckled my boots, zipped my jacket over my chin, and centered my goggles over my helmet. Looking over the edge of the cliff, I spotted the landing area below. It seemed miles away. I had to hit it perfectly to avoid the jagged rocks lurking below the fluffy snow.

After scouting the jump and the take-off spot and deciding it was doable, Derek went around the cliff to take a video of my jump.

I patted down the deep snow approximately thirty feet from the cliff's edge to make sure my take-off would be smooth, so I could jump out far enough to clear the rocks.

Fear was ever-present while I waited for the go-ahead. My heart continued to pound while Derek got himself into position to record my epic jump.

People from the Kuma lift rooted me on, and I did my best to breathe and not let my legs shake. I skied toward the cliff, seeing treetops covered with snow below me. The reality of the jump was more frightening than I had imagined.

"Go get it, D Mac!" Derek shouted, giving me the go-ahead.

The time had come; there was no going back.

I quickly flung my skis, body, and spirit off the cliff's cornice toward the crystal-blue sky that awaited me. Airborne for two seconds, I felt like an eagle for about fifty feet. There was not a sound while I was in flight.

Landing in powdery snow, I looked up and heard cheering.

I'd conquered my goal! And that fine moment would not have been possible without setting the goal in the first place.

Goals are mandatory for achieving success. Otherwise, you are like a sailboat without a rudder, meandering about and drifting aimlessly in the sea.

Goals are necessary for people who are achievement-oriented and driven to succeed. But even people who are not as driven, who are happy doing their own thing, can benefit from setting goals, though their goals might look quite different from an entrepreneur's goals.

There is no right or wrong when it comes to your goals. The important thing is to set them with a firm grasp on who you are and what you want to achieve.

Do You Need Goals?

If you are 100% satisfied with every aspect of your life right now, feel free to skip ahead to the next chapter. If you are driven to climb higher and higher in all aspects of your life and are seeking a deeper level of satisfaction, setting and achieving goals will help you achieve success.

Many people routinely set goals around December 31st to plan for the new year, and then don't revisit them until the following year to see how they did. This is not an effective way to achieve your goals and get the things you want out of the process.

A better approach is to develop goals that are meaningful to you throughout the year. An effective way to determine what goals to set is through journaling. Carry a small notebook around with you and write about the things you want out of life. Journal about why you want them and why they are important to you. Now, when you set goals, you'll create better, more meaningful, and energizing targets for yourself.

Smart Goals

Smart goals are goals that are specific, measurable, achievable, relevant, and time-bound. Goals that hit all these areas are more likely to be met.

Specific

To achieve a goal, you need to know exactly what you're shooting for. Without a target, you are shooting blind. Let's say you want to lose weight. Instead of saying, "I want to lose weight," say, "I want to lose twenty-five pounds," or, "I want to weigh 175 lbs." Being specific clearly identifies your target, and our brains love to work with specifics and know the score.

Measurable

When you have a specific target, you create a goal that can be measured because you know your starting point and the desired ending point. With the example of losing weight, you can track your progress and know when you hit your goal. If you start at 200 lbs. and are now at 180, you know where you stand. Based on the amount of time it took to lose the first twenty pounds, you will have a clear idea of how much time it will take to lose the last five.

Achievable and audacious

It's important to set some goals that are easily achievable because they allow you to start experiencing success with goal setting. Little victories build confidence, but it is also important to challenge yourself a bit by setting bigger, audacious goals. Push yourself out of your comfort zone to stretch and grow.

In general, most of your goals should make you feel a little uncomfortable and not sure you will achieve them. Don't get discouraged if you don't meet your lofty aspirations because the real magic comes from the person you become while you chase down your goals.

Relevant

Ask yourself why each goal you set is important to you. Why does it send chills down your spine at the thought of achieving it? Why does it keep coming up over and over in your life? Find the relevance because it is the key element in the goal-setting process. When the going gets tough, it's easy to blow off irrelevant goals for something easier and more readily available.

Time-Bound

Having a specific period to work with keeps you and your goals on track. Otherwise, one month turns into two months and two months into three. Other events and demands on your time will begin to take over and fill in those gaps. Before you know it, another year has gone by, leaving you no closer to your goal. Do this enough, and you'll become discouraged.

When it comes to timeframes, think about your major goals on an annual basis. December 31st is as good a day as any to start. Some people like to set yearly goals on their birthdays. You could start today. Set something up on your schedule and stick to it.

Once your goals are established (incorporating all the smart elements), break them down by establishing quarterly, monthly, and weekly goals. Quarterly goals give you a more manageable target to hit, yet still cause you to stretch. If you miss the mark in one quarter, you have time to get back on track. The same holds true for your monthly and weekly goals when you dial them down into daily tasks.

Finally, get in the habit of planning your week in advance. Look at the calendar for next week before Monday arrives, so you know what you plan to accomplish each day during the week to help hit your monthly, weekly, and daily goals. By looking at your schedule in advance, you will have a clear picture of how much you will be able to do. This helps break things down into manageable pieces, setting expectations and reducing stress because you'll know you are on track and have a handle on things.

Outrageous Goals

I challenge you to scare the bejeezus out of yourself on occasion by setting an outrageous goal, one that pushes you so far out of your comfort zone that it scares the crap out of you. This is where real growth occurs—when you give yourself permission to imagine such exciting targets. Regardless of the outcome, you will never be the same when you push the envelope. You will have expanded your thinking and belief in what is possible and burned the bridge leading back to the old you in the process.

I am a huge fan of the late Jim Rohn. He inspired my life in so many ways with his philosophies on the value of action, moving forward, and developing the person you become along the way. Jim said, "The major value in life is not what you get. The major value in life is who you become in the pursuit of your goals."

In other words, life is not about the destination; it's all about the journey. This is where life happens, in those little moments while you're traveling from goal to goal.

Push yourself to set an outrageous goal on occasion. The person you become in the process of thinking about your goal and while taking the steps required to make it happen will help you become someone who demonstrates courage by facing fear and moving forward anyway. This person is more likely to try something new and different with greater confidence, discipline, and humility.

Sharing Your Goals

Goals should be shared with the important people in your life. This creates accountability.

If you have a goal and keep it to yourself, then don't achieve it, the only person who knows the truth is you. This might seem like a safer bet, but it can work against you. When you don't share your goal and don't achieve it, your personal integrity takes a hit without any support or input from your circle of family and friends who might be able to share some insights and encouragement that will help you try again.

On your own, you might begin developing a bad habit of not hitting your goals. If you are a goal setter, you are either in the habit of hitting your goals, or you are in the habit of not hitting them. The same holds true for pretty much everything. You're in the habit of working out, or you're in the habit of not working out. Being in the habit of not doing something sets the stage for creativity with your excuses and ushers in the blame game. That's never good.

We are resilient beings, capable of tolerating quite a bit of discomfort before we make a change. Often, we wait until the pain of not doing anything different exceeds the pain of making a change. Before acting, we tend to slowly raise our threshold of denial and learn to become more comfortable with lackluster results. Sharing your goals with other people tends to nip this in the bud and keep us on track. Sharing also makes your goals seem more real and do-able, even the outrageous ones.

Having an accountability partner or partners helps keep you in line and reminds you of your timeline. Your accountability partner is not emotionally invested in the goal itself but is invested in your relationship and in helping you stay true to your word and live with integrity. In short, an honest accountability partner will call us out on our bullshit. I suggest you find like-minded people to collaborate with you and help hold your feet to the flame.

Write and Review

Reviewing goals is another essential part of the goal-setting process. Write your goals down, post them where you can see them, and review them regularly.

One of the primary reasons for writing your goals is accountability. Unless you write them down, goals often get lost in one's imagination. *Did I really say that? When did I say it would happen?*

As human beings, we are incredibly malleable and creative when it comes to making excuses and denial. Especially when nobody else knows we're doing it. If it's just us who gets hurt, we'll adjust our threshold of pain and denial upward a bit and learn to adapt and get comfortable with this new level of mediocrity. It seems odd, but that approach seems easier for some people than the effort of accomplishing their goals to begin with.

Denial, regret, and excuses seem incredibly taxing and energy-intensive to me. How about you? It's far easier to set yourself up for success with good habits.

Outside my office is a whiteboard where my goals are listed. I see them daily as I walk by. A vision board is another effective way to create a daily reminder of your goals. You can post written goals and images that support them. Saving the file and images into a folder called "Goals," then setting your computer screen saver to that folder is another clever way to put your goals in front of yourself regularly. Write your goals on Post-its and stick them around your house and in your car.

This might seem like a lot of extra work, but the small amount of effort required to post your goals in multiple places pays huge dividends in programming your subconscious mind. Ideally, you will be able to recite your goals to anyone, at any time, without hesitation. This ensures your subconscious mind knows them and is always working in the background, even while you sleep, to achieve them.

Different Goals, Different Areas of Life

Now that you understand the basic goal-setting process, you can set goals for the areas of your life you wish to grow. You may only want to focus on one or two areas like professional and finance, or you could apply goals to all areas of your life. I prefer to break things down into what I call the "train of life."

To do this, think about who you are and the many different roles you play each day, professionally and personally. There is no way you could fit all of these roles on a business card—husband, father, brother, son, investor, sales executive, teammate, author, speaker, trainer, philanthropist, extreme skier, traveler, wild n' crazy guy. The list goes on and on for me, and I'm sure it does for you too.

Breaking things down into your train of life compartments helps you organize the many sides of your life into key areas so you can focus on your dreams and desires individually.

When areas of your life are a priority, they are inline. Like a train, they start with the engine and end with the caboose.

Being aware of what's important to you at certain times in your life allows you to be more focused and efficient, setting one or more goals in those relevant areas. Sometimes, you're better off putting all your fuel into the engine, for example. Other times, you want to spread that energy around the whole train or enjoy the ride from the caboose.

Thinking about your priorities this way helps you become clear about what matters to you as you find patterns and narrow your focus to each area you wish to address. Areas that are on the train but are not in alignment with your values can get kicked back to the caboose or off the train altogether instead of hitching a free ride!

It's easy to neglect certain aspects of your life while you are busy attending to other, more pressing matters like making money and keeping a roof over your head. In particular, the more intangible areas like spirituality, love, relationships, and personal development tend to suffer and take a backseat when we're busy working or out changing the world. But these parts of life are important too. In some ways, maybe they are the most important of all. That's one of the best parts about goals—you get to decide what means the most to you, and you can change your focus anytime to make your goals work for you.

I use the following trains, always chugging along, in my planning. You might have others that work better for you, so feel free to change the labels and add or subtract from this list:

- Love
- Relationships
- Health
- Wealth
- Contribution
- Spirituality
- Personal/Self
- Travel/Adventure

The Goals/Success Correlation

The most successful people tend to have very defined goals. They hold themselves accountable, and they have peer groups who hold them accountable too. They review their goals regularly and work their way through planned courses of action to achieve them. If they are stuck, they step back, re-evaluate, and set a new course of action. These people are passionate about what they are doing and relentless in the pursuit of their goals.

In contrast, people who are not as successful often don't have goals or anyone to hold them accountable and seem to float along through life without any sense of purpose or responsibility. They will argue that they don't want the added pressure of achieving goals, and they tend to shoot from the hip in a moment-by-moment way of being.

"I don't need the added stress," they say. "I'm fine with where I'm at."

This way of life seems perfectly fine for some people and is a choice they consciously make. But when their lack of goals and direction becomes a problem, these people often complain about their situation.

You can do the work of goal setting and work toward goals, or you can do the work of complaining, wringing your hands, and floundering about, looking for solutions when life doesn't go your way.

Missing the Mark

Let's say there's one day left in the month, and you are miles away from hitting your sales or income goal. You might be tempted to change your goal, lowering it, so you hit it. If you set a goal for ego's sake and your reasons are more about vanity or keeping score, then don't adjust your goal. Deal with missing the mark instead. Then, revisit the reasons you missed your goals without making excuses. Take responsibility and don't pass the blame to anyone else for not meeting your desired outcome. Set up a new plan for next month and keep forging forward.

When you establish a goal, you should consider several factors, all of which are supported by deeper meaning and purpose. If you set a goal to make X dollars this month, you most likely plan to use that money for specific things, all of which are meaningful to you. You can use these desires as fuel for your motivation.

You can also use the consequences of missing your target to propel you forward no matter how many times you come up short. Missing your mark means you will feel some pain in certain areas. This might be missing out on events or activities, the added stress of not making ends meet, or having other people close to you feel let down or disappointed.

Two of the greatest sources of motivation are pleasure and pain. The easiest way to avoid the pain of not hitting a goal is not to set a goal in the first place! This is the main reason many people don't set goals or don't achieve at the level they are capable of operating. They are avoiding the pain they associate with potential failure. But there is a better way.

When you come up short on a goal, look at the positives and what you accomplished in the process. If you set a goal to contribute $1,000 to charity this month and only managed to give $500, you still gave five hundred dollars. The organization you supplied the money to will be able to help other people that much more. Half is way better than zero, right?

By simply changing your perspective and language from "I failed" to "I am that much farther ahead than I was without my goal," you'll be able to regroup, step back from your goal, and recalibrate for the next month or quarter.

Look at what happened and where you got off track. Examine your reasons for setting this goal in the first place and the consequences of not making it. Then, energize yourself to go for it again using a new plan.

Pay Now or Pay Later

Achieving a goal is a form of pleasure. Good feelings make revisiting and reviewing your goals, especially your *whys*, powerful. Every time you visualize what life will be like when you hit your targets, you'll feel empowered and enjoy a positive rush. This is important because hitting your goals requires discipline and well-thought-out habits. You'll need to put some effort in on the front end, but you'll pay now and reap the rewards later.

The flipside is doing nothing right now, floating along and simply getting by. By avoiding the pain of setting goals or the pain you associate with failing, you set yourself up for future regrets.

The real killer here is time. In certain areas of your life, time can be a more pressing factor than in others—your wealth and finances are prime examples. This is true when it comes to investing for your retirement because of the time value of money. Your health is another time-sensitive area—we're all dying from the moment we're born. Not to be a downer, but it's true; we're not getting any younger, and if we don't take care of ourselves now, it might come back to haunt us later.

Invest time and energy early and enjoy the bounty and pleasures of your efforts for the rest of your life. Or suffer the pain later in the form of regrets, struggles, and challenges.

Which pain do you prefer—discipline or regret?

If you'd like better odds at pleasure, set goals.

But You Hate Goalsetting

If you are like many people, currently not setting goals because you dislike even the idea of goal setting, you likely have some issue with responsibility. Everyone struggles with this at one time or another. I did for many years, and it took some soul-searching to come around to the whole idea of goal setting.

To overcome this hurdle, think about a goal that is important to you. Focus on what you want and why. Imagine how it will feel to have what you want. Zero-in on what makes you happy, what brings you joy, and what makes you light-up on the inside when you think about it. You know yourself better than anyone, so don't be afraid to take an honest assessment and shoot for what you truly desire.

Imagine the pleasure you'll feel when you achieve this goal. You can use this feeling to get in the habit of seeking that pleasure, using the motivation you achieved from earlier chapters and exercises to propel you into setting goals with a new outlook.

Reverse Engineering Goals

Breaking a goal down into smaller, bite-sized pieces is a fantastic way to boost your motivation and fuel your efforts. For example, this past year, I set a sales goal of generating 300,000 gross profit dollars in a month (over 1 million in sales dollars), which some time ago was hard to fathom.

A dollar amount, though, is just a number. Depending on the industry you're in, this figure could be astronomical, or it could be peanuts. For me, this figure represented a bit of a stretch. I felt uneasy, and my brain came up with all kinds of what-if scenarios, working overtime, trying to protect me from the pain of failure.

To get past this and onto the business of generating a million dollars in sales for the month, I reverse-engineered my scary, uncertain goal, chunking it down into more attainable pieces. I looked at my monthly sales average and calculated what the goal increase would be over my proven track record. This turned my million-dollar goal into a few-hundred-thousand-dollar goal. My brain found this much more manageable.

Working with this new, more palatable number, I reviewed my accounts. I looked at my top customers and did the math. What if I increased sales by 5%-10% with each of them? How about the rest of my clients? Could I do 3%-5% more in sales with them? I decided on a plan that included calling on and closing one new, big client. I also thought about other customers who could be converted from one part of my business to another. The more I examined the "problem," the more solutions I found, and the easier the goal became in my mind. Since starting with a good attitude is key, this propelled me forward with confidence. I blew past that goal and set a new audacious goal that I am still working on.

By starting with the end in mind and reverse engineering

backward, I made the numbers more manageable and less stressful. With each smaller chunk conquered, your mind will begin to see how sweet success is, and you will be motivated to work even harder and more creatively to reach the next goal.

Use this technique for any goal you set, especially your crazy, outrageous goals. Set your target, then work backward to draft your plan for hitting it.

Work smarter. One can be the hardest worker around but not the most efficient and productive if they are not using their resources or focusing on the traditional 80/20 rule. Remember, 80% of your business will come from the top 20% of your clients.

Utilize your time appropriately to grow your business or network.

Identifying and Overcoming Obstacles

There are always obstacles and challenges on the path to your goals. You can embrace them by changing the way you view them and what you say about them, or you can use challenges as an excuse to quit.

When we hit a roadblock, it's natural for one of the practical solutions to be "I give up." This is a magical solution that offers instant gratification by turning you down the path of least resistance until you run into the overwhelming traffic jam created by everyone already on that road. While you're stuck in gridlock, you'll have plenty of time to beat yourself up for quitting.

Take a better, less-traveled road, and avoid the pain that almost always comes when we give in to the temptation to give up on ourselves. Whether you sidestep challenges or bulldoze right over them, each time you take action, you prove to yourself that you are unstoppable. Problems? No problem!

When you encounter obstacles, pay attention to the words you use to describe them. Do they include negative ones like can't, won't, and don't? Are you complaining or using obstacles and challenges as reasons to bail on your goals? Be honest.

We all get frustrated. When this happens, go to a private place where you can have a good rant. Be emotional, loud, and unfiltered. Don't hold back. It is better to let these feelings out than to leave them bottled up inside. Others might prefer to go for a run or to the gym. Doing something physical lets any stress or bad emotions out.

We all need to blow off steam on occasion so we can come back feeling more positive.

When you're ready, shift gears and funnel your remaining energy into changing your perspective. Strive to view every obstacle, problem, and challenge you face working toward your goal as a blessing. Try writing your challenges out, reframing them, and listing the possible positives. It might be hard at first, but you can almost always find some silver-lining in every obstacle.

It's important to remember that challenges are gifts given only to select people who dare to do what you are in the process of doing. Obstacles are there to help mold your soul. Be grateful because these temporary roadblocks are opportunities to review what you are doing and reconnect with your reasons for doing them.

Figuring Things Out as You Go

We've been talking a bunch about being organized and systematic with the goal-setting process. But it's important to build in some flexibility so you can operate without a plan too when needed.

Often, the best path is individual, depending on the person and the period in their life. For example, my wife and I love to travel. We often head over to Europe or other places around the world and prefer to follow a loose plan, figuring things out as we go. We pull up Airbnb and see what looks good and embrace the mystery of what might be around the next corner.

Now that we've had our first child, we've made some adjustments to our lifestyle and the routines that we previously held rigidly in-line with our goals. We don't go to the gym as often, and we don't participate in the variety of sports we used to due to time constraints; however, this is okay because a new set of priorities took over, and our daily routine needed to shift. These changes fit with our overall priorities in life and with who we want to be at our cores.

This important target is everchanging for all of us. Being realistic about your lifestyle and aware of your chapter of life is important when it comes to goal setting.

Be flexible. Be aware. Do the work to make awareness possible and try not to do so much that you end up killing yourself and your happiness in the process.

Success Goals vs. Fulfillment Goals

Many people measure success by looking at finances. Unfortunately, money doesn't always equate to emotional fulfillment, and it's easy to get stuck on a figure-eight loop where fulfillment seems elusive. You can knock out all the business goals in the world and still be unhappy if you haven't balanced work and home, money, and soul-riches.

We've talked about this a bit and will visit the topic in-depth in a later chapter. For now, don't fall into the trap of holding off happiness until you make millions of dollars or buy a new yacht. Strive to set goals that fulfill you in the short term too.

I'm not discounting the importance of financial success. But looking at life and goals as about more than money will go a long way to keeping your boat afloat and sailing strong. Taking care of your fundamental needs will give you the freedom to master your deeper self. Emotional fulfillment is a deeper, richer target to shoot for in life.

Start by looking inward and loving yourself first. If you have an open and loving heart, people will be attracted to you, and you'll be able to genuinely share with the world around you and feel successful in life.

Keys:

Success without a plan isn't possible.

You're not going to reach Hawaii in a sailboat without a chart of the Pacific Ocean. Sure, there might be a small percentage of people who could do it, but even if they made it, the journey would take a lot longer. For 99.9% of us, having a plan is essential.

Accept your starting point.

We can't set goals without knowing and accepting our starting point. Before you can concentrate on the finish line or on desired outcomes, you need to know your current situation so you can work out a solid plan of action. Be realistic, and make sure you don't make it better or worse than it is.

Do the best you can.

Measure yourself against your own capabilities and past performances. Create benchmarks, set goals, and work with your abilities to determine your unique definition of success.

Learn the fundamental keys to success.

- Passion
- Vision
- Purpose (what you want and why you want it)
- Attitude
- Model (Who's already done it?)
- Goals (Build a passion for them.)
- Master your inner dialogue and self-talk.

- Leverage the power of the internet.
- Personal development (Be ready to try new things and fail.)
- Persistence and resilience
- Work/Life balance

 **Tools:**

Know your GPA!

In school, your GPA reflects where you stand and your efforts to date. Rate yourself from 1 to 10 (1 = needs work 10 = you're cruising) on each of the following three areas:

- **GOAL** – What result or outcome do you want? Be specific in detail and include the time your goal will take to achieve.

- **PURPOSE** – Why do you want it? The more whys, the better! Your whys are the leverage you need to get moving and keep moving when the going gets tough.

- **ACTION** – What steps and actions have you taken toward your desired goal? What steps and actions do you plan to take, and in what order will you take them?

CHAPTER 5

Master Your Inner-Dialogue.

I can speak to my soul only when the two of us are off exploring deserts or cities or mountains or roads.

Paulo Coelho

We all have internal self-talk, running dialog in our heads. Often, this commentary is negative unless we train our minds to know that everything that happens in life is meant to serve us for the better.

With this foundation of belief, we can ask better quality questions of ourselves that empower us.

We also must realize that thoughts are not facts; they are just the brain's way of dealing with the world. Just because you think something doesn't make it true or worth spending time mulling over.

Many useless thought patterns include questions like "Why am I not good enough? Why can't I be happy? Why this, or why that?" We can easily take a fact like Mary isn't smiling and turn it into Mary isn't smiling because she doesn't like me. Mary is my boss. If she's not smiling, I must have done something wrong. I'm going to be fired. What will I do for money? Everything following the fact (Mary is not smiling) is just a thought, a random function of the brain.

Change the paradigm and handle negative thought spirals by asking yourself questions like, "What is the blessing in this? What is it I don't see? How can this serve me and inspire others right now? What is the blessing in disguise?"

Consciously address your thoughts and tell them to hush if they are not serving you. Learn to separate fact from fiction and cultivate habits that encourage positive thought patterns. Focus on changing debilitating questions that often begin with "why" to empowering, solution-oriented questions that often begin with "how" or "what."

Mindset is Everything

Your mindset controls your life in multiple ways, so your thoughts control your destiny. Letting your thoughts roam free can lead to distraction or can deter you from moving forward, sending you off in the wrong direction, down the wrong path, so you never reach your dreams or your destiny.

Think of thoughts as a central, governing body that guides us throughout our lives. It's up to us to develop strong mindsets that will help us achieve our goals and develop a vision for our lives.

What Do You Say When You Talk to Yourself?

Negative self-talk always causes you to think poorly of yourself, others, and situations you find yourself dealing with. We all think negative thoughts sometimes, especially in times of stress or turmoil. I was guilty of this after I was cut six times from sport's teams during my first two years in high school.

At the time, these events took charge of my thoughts and messed with my mindset, causing me to feel horrible about myself. I felt rejected. Even though I knew I was good enough, someone had told me I wasn't, and I experienced a central fear everyone has at times—I am not loved because I am not good enough.

Emotionally negative thoughts seem to lead to the worst and most destructive self-talk. Most people want to feel a sense of belonging and love in their lives.

Fortunately, I found a way to squash my negative thoughts and funneled my efforts into other sports and activities. I also learned a valuable lesson about how to process feedback, words, and opinions from outside sources. This led to the following three declarations to help support a positive mindset and a more peaceful and positive existence:

1. Only I decide what everything means when it comes to my results and experiences.
2. Everything that happens can have a positive connotation.
3. I know and believe everything that comes into my mind is there to serve me.

There are times when I must dig a little deeper to find positives and understand the deeper meaning behind events. To do this, I am willing to try new viewpoints to help me see different perspectives. This is something I encourage everyone to do when faced with challenges and situations that seem black and white. Change your perspective. Put on a new pair of mental bifocals and make the conscious decision to look at the troubling situation in new ways. When you do this, your only mission is to find a different take on things. It can help to pretend you're slipping on a pair of 3D glasses that enable you to see beyond the obvious.

Your success begins with your self-talk. Once you take the reins, you will find self-talk is easily led. Running on autopilot is what leads to trouble.

Control the controllable.

We've all read books that tell us it's important to do this or do that to improve our lives. But let's go beyond that because, while awareness is certainly the beginning of the process of changing, to make change happen, you need to know where and how to focus your attention and what steps to take. What do you need to do, and how do you do it?

Check your fab four.

Your body structure, self-talk, focus, and faith (your fab four) are all interconnected.

Structure is often the easiest to see, so begin to take charge of your thoughts by looking at yourself in the mirror, paying attention to your body. Are your shoulders slumped? Are you slouching or walking funny? Do you feel aches and pains you don't normally feel? Indicators like headaches, backaches, and tight shoulders are clear signals of stress and negative energy flowing within your body.

When a negative thought comes into your mind, make a conscious effort to pull your shoulders back, tighten your core, and stand up strong and straight while taking solid, deep breaths.

It's amazing how powerful it is to change your body structure and how quickly doing so will shift your focus. When you change your focus, your inner dialogue changes. Try it as you look into a mirror. Some people find this works best when they assume a superhero stance, with arms raised powerfully in the air and legs strong beneath them. The point is to shift your body out of its slump and communicate different messages to your brain. Changing any of the fab four immediately affects the others.

Changing your body structure is the fastest, easiest change to make, so when you catch yourself slumping, straighten up. If you're frowning, smile. With the people you love, do the same. Smile at them. Smile at strangers when you're out in public. As simple as it seems, this behavior will add a little bounce to your step and make you feel better on the inside, which always leads to a shift in focus and more positive self-talk.

If you are sitting in a chair and your mind is swirling around a bunch of negative thoughts, get up and go for a walk. Take your dog for a walk if you have a dog, or simply stand up and get your body moving. In an instant, your focus will shift because your environment has changed. The scenery changes, the sun warms your body, the wind blows across your face, birds are chirping. Get the picture?

The foundation of your fab four is structure. The shifts you make externally directly influence your body internally. Work on that first and watch your perspective expand as you enjoy fast change and newfound control over yourself.

Ask focusing questions.

One of the best questions to ask yourself during a challenging or emotional situation is, "What's great about this right now?" Think about how the situation can serve you and inspire you to move to the next level. Look for what could be magical about your dilemma and think about how you can use it to your advantage.

We've talked about this before, but it's worth revisiting as we discuss the value of directing your self-talk with better questions designed to banish negative voices and help you regain focus.

Ask yourself what you might not be seeing about your situation that could help you change things so you can respond differently than you have in the past. By choosing to look at things from a different perspective, you can reduce the stress you may be feeling and put a stop to getting more worked-up as your mind begins to swirl and lead you down a dark, emotional path.

There are incredibly difficult challenges many people face that call for a deeper discussion here. Losing a loved one, being diagnosed with a terminal illness, losing a limb or faculty that leaves you permanently disabled are a few examples. Asking, "What's great about this?" might seem overly simplistic. In extreme cases, the approach should focus more on changing your perspective. After all, if you're tackling something serious, isn't it best to do it from a place of peace rather than one of turmoil? Perhaps you can't change what's happening, but you will manage it better with the right frame of mind.

In these cases, ask yourself questions like "How else can I view this situation?" or "How have other people handled this challenge in ways I admire?" You might never fully come around to find what's great about a tragedy or debilitating illness, but you can embrace the power you have and choose to move forward in ways that serve you the best.

Regardless of the circumstances, nobody can take away our ability to decide how we view what comes next. The power to choose our focus is huge. Sharing your experiences with others when you've gone through this process and come out the other side in a better place lets you lead by example and further strengthens your faith in yourself. Faith is the X-factor that will get you through to the finish line.

Everything counts, but nothing matters.

The goal of asking empowering questions is to move to a different, healthier place than you are currently. For example, if you take your car to the dealership for an oil change, and they give it back to you with damage to the bumper and front-end you didn't notice until you got home, you have a choice to make. You can get angry and call the dealer in a rage, fester, and boil in it for the entire weekend, poisoning your mood and possibly jeopardizing your chances of achieving a positive outcome with the service manager at the dealer. Or you can casually take a few pictures of the damage, call your service guy, and hand everything over to them. Peacefully, you have a conversation instead of attacking people. *Accidents happen, people make mistakes*, you tell yourself. *This will all work out.* Take a deep breath, breathing in peace and exhaling love, letting all of it go. No matter what happens next, you will move forward like a powerful, honest human being who lives with integrity and grace. And you will go about your business, enjoying your weekend, knowing in the grand scheme of things, everything counts, but nothing matters.

Consistently Positive Self-Talk

As I have become more in touch with my personal development, I have used various techniques to improve my inner dialogue.

I post goals where I can see them, and I read them aloud regularly. I routinely look at myself in the mirror and say, "You've got this!" before a big meeting. I also use a powerful technique I learned from Napoleon Hill, author of *Think and Grow Rich*, called autosuggestion. Before I go to sleep at night, I review my goals, and then I visualize having already achieved them. I also verbalize positive identity statements that begin with "I am." These statements reflect who I am and reinforce the things I need to do to get what I want out of life and be the person I am meant to be. For example, I might say, "I am powerful. I am love. I am passionate. I am courageous. I am unstoppable."

Try it. It's a wonderful way to end your day and drift off to sleep feeling energized by reinforcing your own power and goodness.

Some nights, I read a book to relax. Other nights, I review my goals and say my identity statements. There are also nights where I want to be with my beautiful wife or close my eyes and just go to sleep. That's okay. I do the things I'm sharing with you to the best of my abilities, but I'm not perfect. I don't expect you to be either. Consistency is the key. Whatever that looks like for you is fine.

This is where striving to be your best over the long haul comes into play. When you positively talk to yourself as much as possible whenever you catch yourself thinking and saying negative things, you stand the greatest chance of changing your life for the better.

Change and improvement happen gradually. Most people overestimate what they can achieve in a shorter time frame but underestimate what they can achieve over a longer period if they stay consistent. Hit singles and doubles; there is no need to try and try and hit a home run. Strive for a consistent and sustainable rise over time.

Positive Self-Talk in Tough Times

From 2004 to 2006, I invested in real estate in California,

Nevada, and Texas. I bought homes and used the rise in appreciation value to leverage my way into a real estate portfolio. In the beginning, my net worth, at least on paper, grew significantly. My confidence and my identity soared when I became a millionaire in just a few years.

I planned to sell my single-family property portfolio after a few years and invest the profits into apartment buildings. Then, 2008 arrived, and the bubble burst very quickly.

The value of the homes I had bought began to fall. And fall. And fall. Buying and renting properties to fund the outstanding mortgages had worked like a well-oiled machine, but in 2008, I developed a serious cash-flow problem. Home values fell way below what I had paid, rents were not covering my mortgage payments, and many renters had their own financial issues, prompting them to skip paying their rent altogether. Selling at a loss only put me deeper in the hole, and everything snowballed.

I hung on and scrambled to stay afloat, spending hours on the phone every day, negotiating and meeting with banks, seeking to change my loans to obtain more manageable interest rates. Many days were spent running to the post office to send legal correspondence for bank refinancing options while also doing my best to grow my corporate, 100% commission-based sales territory.

This was time-consuming, overwhelming, and stressful.

Though my bank account took a hard hit, the hardest blow of all was to my identity and feelings of self-worth. I went from being on top of the world to feeling lower than the dirt under a dog turd in the yard. Yet, I look back with pride at how I managed things and the efforts I made to hang in there. Though those were some of the darkest times in my life, I managed to keep reminding myself that I was a good person with a good heart who was going to be okay no matter what.

In 2012, after riding the storm out for as long as I could, I filed for bankruptcy.

Despite the lows, those turbulent four and a half years yielded amazing, positive changes in my life.

My sales career took a hit in 2013 when two of my top accounts were lost in account acquisitions. This equaled 25% of my portfolio; however, I was determined never to be a victim again.

Very soon after making this mindset change, my business started to take off. Most importantly, I met my amazing wife, Laura, in Texas. This led to the most wonderful, positive changes in my life—marriage and my beautiful baby girl, Mila. My wife and daughter blow my mind daily with their unconditional love.

My commitment to personal development also helped me weather the storm, and I learned an unbelievably valuable lesson—to always train my mind to expect the best while preparing for the worst. I read personal development books and listened to audio programs to carry me over the peaks and troughs of life like a sailboat navigating through a storm in the ocean. When you're facing fifty-foot waves, from crest to trough, it's pure terror. Then, the storm breaks, and it's smooth sailing again. What makes all the difference in handling the storms of life is putting positive vibes and messages into your emotional bank account.

I survived my dark times by continuing to believe in myself and positively talk to myself, investing time to attend seminars and workshops with Tony Robbins and other inspirational leaders to reinforce my own identity and keep moving forward. I increased my involvement even more by leading personal development workshops, helping others to keep moving and growing despite obstacles.

There is power in helping other human beings. No matter how big or small the challenge, when you help someone else, you wind up feeling better in the process. The next time you face an obstacle in your life, spend some time lending a helping hand to someone else. Shift your focus from your own woes and problems to another person in need, another cause outside of yourself. You will heal faster, feel better, boost your own confidence and self-worth while possibly making new, quality friends in the process.

The Importance of a Flexible Self-Identity

There are times when you will need to change course, admit defeat, or abandon ship. One of the keys to moving forward after a setback is making an honest examination of your efforts and your desire to live with integrity about the decisions you make. You can't just abandon your goals when things get tough. But, sometimes, you must abandon a goal and realign yourself for well-thought-out reasons or because you've changed destinations. This is okay.

If you need help, find people, whether family or not, who can be honest with you even when honesty might sting. Tell them what's going on and listen to what they have to say.

My dad, and my stepfather, Steve Diamond, are two highly trusted confidants of mine. They can offer advice on a wide range of subjects from various perspectives, and their ability to be brutally honest has rubbed off on me over the years. Whenever I am in doubt or need advice, I pick up the phone and start asking away!

Most decisions involve an emotional part and an analytical one. The ability to examine your options and think things through builds confidence and an ability to make decisions and get behind them. In the bigger picture, analytical ability is a significant part of inner peace. It prevents you from constantly second-guessing yourself, even when you must change course because of obstacles.

Regardless of your outcomes, doing your best to make things work and achieve your goals will always help you deal with setbacks in healthy ways. Knowing you did all you could before deciding to leave a project will make all the difference when it comes to picking up the pieces and moving on when the storm is over. Doing your best while immersed in a project or activity is a positive recipe for living life with no regrets.

People who always kept moving forward, no matter what, were Dick Hoyt and his son, Rick. Together they were known as "Team Hoyt." They took part in dozens of triathlons and Ironman competitions together. Rick is a quadriplegic. His mother and father, Dick and Judy Hoyt, ignored doctors who told them Rick should be institutionalized when he was young. They fought to put him through public school and college, making countless sacrifices over their lives. When Rick was fifteen, he asked his thirty-six-year-old father if they could run a race together. Soon, the focus of the question shifted from "if" to "how." The mindset they shared became all about moving around and over obstacles. Together, they created custom wheelchairs, bicycle sidecars, and small kayaks that Rick could use. After the 2014 Boston Marathon, their final event as Team Hoyt, they had taken part in over 400 marathons, runs, and Ironman events. Their success can be traced back to and began with one thing—a positive and flexible mindset.

Keys:

- Determine your own meanings for everything. You are the master of what anything means.

- Choose to feel a sense of gratitude, freedom, humility, and joy.

Tools:

- **Meditations with incantations and powerful identity statements.** For example, you can say, "I am courage. I am loving. I lead, not follow. I am a force for good. I dance with fear and embrace the unknown! I am guided in my light. I choose my fate."

- **Study the location of your inner dialogue.**

You can't create a solution to something unless you know where it is inside of you. Find where your feelings are in your body. For example, do you feel the impact of your feelings in your gut? Your head? Heart? Or all over? Location matters. As the saying goes, "If you are in your head, you are dead, and, quite the contrary, if you are in your heart, you are smart!" If you feel the impact of your thoughts in your head, you are measuring, comparing, and judging. If you feel them in your heart, you are connecting to a deeper emotional state. If you feel them in your gut, your instincts might be informing you of a future opportunity that may or may not serve you.

When you have a roadmap of the place an issue stems from, you can ask yourself the right, specific, and empowering questions to get yourself out of a funk. Make this a regular practice by checking in with yourself several times throughout your day and using the techniques we discussed in this chapter to alter your body, improve your emotions, and redirect your focus.

CHAPTER 6

Networking and Social Media

You can make more friends in two months by becoming interested in other people than you can in two years by trying to get other people interested in you.

Dale Carnegie

Quite honestly, I didn't want anything to do with social media because I wanted time away from technology. Dealing with a lot of technology in the workplace was enough for me. But I've realized I need to embrace social media to inspire people with my messages and connect with people who inspire me in return. Social media is the new town hall and water cooler.

I'm still a rookie at this game and achieved financial success and emotional fulfillment without it. Yet, this is a new age, and if you don't embrace social media, then many possibilities for growth will pass you by. So, it's important to talk about social media, networking, and your circle of influence to come up with the best ways to navigate this important landscape.

We Get by with a Little Help from Our Friends: Your Circle of Influence

When it comes to individual growth and success in every area of our life, one of the most significant factors is our circle of influence—the people we hang around with. Their input and influence can have a major impact on you (the person you are now and the person you will become in the future).

Your circle of influence consists of members of your immediate family, your peer group, your spouse, girlfriend, boyfriend, your friends, neighbors, and anyone with whom you interact regularly. These relationships are important because they have a direct impact on you and on your level of emotional fulfillment as you journey to the place you want to be in life.

Many people live in challenging households where they don't have a healthy level of support. Others grew up in an environment where they weren't encouraged to succeed. You can still love these people in your family and in your life, but you don't need to stay within this circle and live by other's standards. Yet, deciding to seek better environments and relationships with more positive, forward-thinking individuals can be a tough decision to make.

No matter what your dreams and goals are, one of the best things you can do to achieve them is to surround yourself with people who have walked or are at least farther down the path you want to travel. If you want to be wealthy or financially secure, start hanging around with people who have achieved a higher level of financial success than you currently have. If you want to achieve a greater level of inner peace, cultivate a friendship with your local yoga guru or with a person who is highly in touch with their spiritual side. In today's world, you can connect with anyone online, in groups, or on social media and websites.

When seeking input from people who already have what you want, make sure to look carefully for a balance of material success and emotional fulfillment. Someone financially secure but driven by an overblown ego, who acts like a jerk and has been divorced multiple times, is a person you might want to avoid. Someone who is extremely attractive but lacks character and humility or who is as dumb as a rock will likely be trouble eventually. I encourage you to look for the complete package.

When looking to build your knowledge of money and finance, look for well-balanced people, those who are emotionally and financially well-off. They don't have to be very wealthy, but people with a good handle on finances who make sound financial decisions will serve as good models for character traits you wish to hone.

There is nothing wrong with not having money, especially when you have an abundance of emotional wealth and spirit. But when trying to build wealth, avoid people who are struggling financially, have a negative attitude, or frequently complain, showing stress, hopelessness, and lack of accountability. These characteristics tend to lead to poor habits in other areas too.

One of the primary characteristics I look for in people to add to my circle of influence is good time-management skills. I've noticed a direct correlation between success while living a well-balanced life and efficient time management. Successful people find the time to play and rejuvenate themselves and balance these pursuits with their work and career.

When people effectively manage their time and busy

schedules, stress levels tend to go down, and their level of overall happiness increases. I prefer to hang around tribes of people who are in emotionally happy states.

Inner and Outer Circles of Influence

People who make up your circles of influence touch your lives to different degrees. Some people are direct advisors and help guide you throughout your life, holding your feet to the fire when you need it. They are there for you when the chips are down. Others affect your life to a lesser degree or frequency, yet still play a valuable role.

Picture your circle of influence as an archery target with a bullseye and surrounding rings. The people in the bullseye are your inner circle—your spouse, your immediate family, and closest friends. These are the people you would confide your deepest secrets and concerns in life to.

The next ring is your extended circle—good friends and family you keep in touch with and see regularly but who don't necessarily know what's happening with you daily.

Your outer circle consists of neighbors, co-workers, members of your church, community, and acquaintances you see occasionally and interact with more infrequently. The levels of conversation here are usually more superficial and in-the-moment than ones you have with your inner and extended circle members.

Finally, there are general connections you have with people you might not have met but who share a common interest or belief with you. Think about social media followers you might have connected with because of their link to someone you know at a deeper level. These might be people who follow what you do and support your efforts or people you follow online. Though you do not have a personal relationship with them, they do have a small degree of influence over you.

Trimming the Deadwood

Looking at your circle of influence, you will probably find people at all levels who are challenging for one reason or another. They might have some qualities that benefit you and a host of others that bring you down or can be downright harmful to your wellbeing. Handling people who are members of your inner and extended circles who bring you down can be one of life's tougher jobs. Still, it's always easier to identify problems in other people. We can spot negative behavior and unhealthy habits quickly when it comes to someone else. The ego is at the center of this dilemma, and we all have one.

Some people are hardcore in their belief that you must

cut negative influences out of your life, like trimming the deadwood off a tree, cutting people out of your life to make room for new growth to occur. By clearing out the deadwood, you can add new people who have a more positive influence to offer. Nip bad seeds in the bud before things get worse.

Philosophically, the idea of cutting out the deadwood to make room for new growth works in some areas. If you have an old car and a one-car garage, when you sell your old car, you make room for a newer vehicle. This is a zero-sum game; everything is equally balanced. There is only room for one car.

But it's difficult to have a zero-sum game when you're talking about people with whom you have a relationship, a long history wrapped in experiences, feelings, and emotions. Turning your back on someone overnight will affect you both, possibly leading to greater difficulties with them and other members of your circles. Rather than cutting people out of your life altogether, I advocate limiting your exposure to people you might consider deadwood or negative influences. The exception to this is people who are harmful in physically or emotionally abusive ways. Run, don't walk, as far as you can from these people.

On social media, it's easy to unfollow people, so you don't see their negative messages every day without blocking or unfriending them and risking hurt feelings. Clean up your regularly visited sites and fill your feed with positive influences, cutting the rest.

When evaluating your relationships, look not only for poor individual habits but poor relationship skills. Poor relationships can be difficult to see because of the layers of emotion involved, but they influence your ability to grow and achieve your goals in life. In some cases, you might be involved with people who operate with a scarcity mentality and from a position of limitation and fear. They don't want you to change or grow because they fear you will leave them behind. They also fear having to look closer at themselves and at their level of achievement or mediocrity. Fear and envy often lead to judgment, negative gossip, and other forms of subtle sabotage.

When I was in my late twenties, I went through a phase, hanging out with a party crowd. We constantly went out at night, staying up until the sun came up, partying, and following a path of general destruction. We were all poor members of each other's circle of influence. This behavior went on for two or three years and negatively affected the speed at which my career got going. While I might have been having a good time, I wasn't heading in a direction that worked for me in the long term. This realization led me to step away from this circle and re-direct my life, and I've never looked back.

Limiting Your Exposure

Spending too much time in the sun causes sunburn and can lead to skin cancer. So, you limit your exposure to the sun, especially around noon, and you use plenty of sunscreen. This simple game plan goes a long way to making you more comfortable, so you can live a longer, healthier life. The same approach works with negative influencers. Keep it simple but be deliberate in your approach.

As you move farther away from the bullseye (inner circle of influence), the amount of time you spend with these people becomes less and less. The most effective way I have found to deal with challenging people is to move them out to the next rings, one level at a time. Where they might have been an inner circle member, they are now part of my extended circle. With less frequent and intimate interaction, this could be all that's necessary and the start of a new, healthier relationship for you.

Honesty is the best approach. Have an open conversation with them and invite them to move forward together. Let them know where you are headed in your life and that you have noticed they seem to be on a different or more distant path. I have found the invitation to come along for the ride is a more effective approach with people I love, rather than cutting them out of my life without giving them a chance. They may need this wake-up call as much as you need to say something. Focus on the road ahead and the potential to grow closer and stronger moving forward. They may choose to remain where they are and be completely content with their decision. The important thing is to give them the opportunity by being open and honest. If they prefer things the way they are, you can feel okay moving them to an outer ring, knowing you tried, ready to welcome them back to the inner ring should they have a change of heart later.

There are people I love dearly and have known my entire life who could easily be in my innermost circle. Although we live in the same orchard, one of us is an apple, and the other is an orange. We're connected, yet we see things differently and are motivated by different things. This is one of the beautiful things about being human—we are all unique and can choose to march to the beat of our own drummer. One is no better than the other, simply different. We don't have to be alike to get along or learn from one another. It's only the toxic weeds we need to be mindful of.

We get to choose who gets to be in our inner circle. Choose wisely.

The Social Media Circle of Influence

Not long ago, the foundation of our relationships was built upon personal interaction and direct communication with people. If problems came up, we worked them out with people in person or over the telephone. Phones were used for conversations and didn't command our attention the way modern smartphones do. Today, making a phone call using your smartphone is almost incidental in the scheme of the many apps and modes of communication phones offer. I wish this weren't the case, but it's a sign of the times and the advancement of technology.

Relationships are now primarily built and maintained using text, chat, video, and social media apps. If you want to grow your business and your network, it makes sense to master these new fundamentals and build your online presence. This is an area I am turning my attention to because of the potential global reach social media has to offer.

Social media helps me reach as many people as possible, allowing me to share and seek wisdom and philosophy. To make the most of this incredible opportunity to expand and develop the best circles of influence, I've committed to improving my online presence and addressing my technology shortcomings. Like all self-improvement, this process started with awareness. Goals came next, then acting and actively making changes. Fortunately, I know I will do whatever it takes to make this happen, though I am still in the goalsetting phase.

Rambling on about how you should do this or that, and then not following my own advice would be sad, and I couldn't live with such hypocrisy. You can be my accountability partner by finding me online when you finish reading this book to check my progress.

Know Thyself

My track record and recent history of getting things done are consistent. That helps me be sure, beyond any doubt, that I will act to improve myself concerning technology and social media. Part of my plan is to use the magic of Google to learn more from thought leaders in this area, so I can plan the best ways to continue (modeling and replicating). God bless the internet!

Self-knowledge is a key point for you to consider. This sense of knowing yourself is powerful. Awareness, coupled with good habits and consistent actions, yields positive results, even when you know you are delving into unfamiliar territory. Positive results supply a level of confidence and character that cannot be borrowed or bought. Notice I did not promise perfect or great results; I only promised positive results. At the start of any endeavor, positive results add to your work in progress and compel you to keep moving forward.

We all have areas we need to improve. The trick is doing the work needed to figure yourself out and finding areas to work on. Get in the habit of being real with yourself and taking honest assessments of where you stand in the various areas of your life. Then, take the necessary steps to change your situation in whatever areas that need improvement. I guarantee the energy it takes to act is far less than the energy it takes to live with mediocrity and to manage excuses.

Managing Online Time and Shielding Yourself from Negativity and Time Suck

Knowing when to do things yourself versus hiring a professional is an important part of successfully balancing success with fulfillment, setting a positive example, and living with integrity.

As I'm working on this book, I am also interviewing virtual assistants to help manage my workload. An assistant will help keep my work and life balance in proper equilibrium. Delegation will allow me to use my resources efficiently so I can be super-effective in work and life. Part of my plan is to have my assistant help with my daily, demanding workload as there are only so many hours in a day, and I have many commitments and demands on my time. Time is the most precious commodity we have because one can never get back time once it has passed. We need to seize it!

Scheduling your online time is a good practice. We all know how easily ten minutes online can turn into an hour watching funny videos and reading articles about things we only have a passing interest in. Some apps can help, setting alarms for you as reminders or even turning off your access to certain time-sucking platforms after a set time. There is even an app that will selectively block mentions of anything you set up. For example, a friend of mine uses this to block "politics" because she doesn't want to feel overwhelmed by political news right now. Another friend blocks mentions of her favorite TV show, so she's not lured away from more important endeavors and never has to read a spoiler for episodes she hasn't seen.

You control what you see and who you spend time with online. Be ruthless when it comes to avoiding negative influences online. Use available tools to cull your feeds of things and people who are negative or bring you down and waste your time. Come up with a plan and take charge of your social media landscape until it serves you rather than the other way around. If you need help figuring out how to do this, ask a teenager, a millennial, or your most tech-savvy friend for guidance.

Just like with other areas of your life, managing your social media time and networking endeavors will be most effective with a plan. Set some goals and boundaries for yourself and vow to stick with them. Regularly take stock of where you are and correct your course if you go off track.

Building Rapport (In-Person and Online)

I cannot stress the importance of rapport skills enough. Relationships form the basis of most businesses, and good ones have helped my corporate sales business grow to over eight figures annually.

Knowing how to connect quickly with people from diverse cultures and with a variety of personalities, whether on the phone, in person, or in a boardroom, is crucial. If you are trying to climb the success ladder, this will be done through your performance and relationships. If you have the performance but not the relationships, then most likely, you are out of luck.

People often think they can talk themselves into rapport with someone. Though possible, it is difficult because the words we use only make up 7% of rapport. Ultimately, people like to work with trustworthy people they feel a connection to. When there is tremendous responsiveness between people, rapport is often great. People also feel a sense of rapport with people they like or aspire to be like and with people they share a feeling of commonality with.

Matching and mirroring is a linguistic technique that has become prevalent in the professional and sales worlds. It's a great technique to fast-track rapport by quickly developing a sense of camaraderie. We can dramatically increase our chances of gaining rapport with someone with the use of tonality (high or low), as this is 38% of rapport building. We can also match their voice's tempo (speed), volume (loud or soft), and timbre, which is the quality deriving from a throat or nasal voice. Matching one's breathing is another great technique to put in your tool belt.

You can also build rapport quickly with someone by matching and mirroring their body language because 55% of rapport comes via body language. Notice how they are standing or sitting. Perhaps their left leg is crossed over their right leg, or their arms are crossed, or they make gestures with their hands as they talk. By subtly matching and mirroring their style, you will unconsciously connect with them. If someone is casual and laid back, don't be loud, formal, or fast. Be yourself while paying attention to the messages others send you; these are clues about how they wish to be seen and treated. Being flexible and responsive to the needs of others always opens more doors than being stubborn and self-centered.

Online, the principles of matching and mirroring also apply. Pay attention to the way people write and communicate. If they write one-sentence emails that are direct and to the point, reply in kind. If they are more elaborate and use smiley faces and various emoticons, respond similarly. If they post to social media in a fun manner with pictures of their dog, post a picture of your dog (or the dog you would like to own) to instantly connect on a dog-lover level.

Ten Things Likable People Do

No matter where you go about your business—online or in-person or a little of both—you'll find there are things likable people do regularly that help them connect and build a tribe of followers.

1. They see the best in others.
2. They are kind to others.
3. They love themselves and others.
4. They are courageous.
5. They have integrity.

6. They are authentic.
7. They are hard-working.
8. They are respectful.
9. They are humble.
10. They are resilient.

The Magic, Personal Touch

To build lifelong, positive relationships, make sure to let others know they are particularly important people to you. This is especially valuable for the people in your inner circle, but it applies to your extended circle and outer circles too.

Pick up the phone and keep in touch. Give or send cards or simple gifts to show people you care. These gestures have more impact than words alone. A handwritten note is powerful. It's old-school, and in today's world, it stands out and differentiates you from the masses who rely on text messages.

The personal touch is the magic touch, so be a magician. Look around for inspiration. Often, you'll find friends or mentors you can model to develop the skills you want in your life. For me, one of these people is Chuck Hogan, one of my partners in a personal development platform. Your Best Life Strategists brings together high-level life and transformational business strategists with individuals and companies to accelerate desired outcomes.

Chuck is the kind of guy who focuses on his family and other people tremendously and not just on himself. Not a day goes by that Chuck does not call his wife and children to tell them he loves them and to express his gratitude for them, making sure they know how important they are to him.

When he developed testicular cancer, he decided it wasn't going to get the best of him or slow him down in any way. He set his fears aside and focused on the positive aspects of his life and the world around him.

Chuck embodies love and shares that love with everyone he meets. He's the type of person I aspire to be and someone I believe is worth emulating in his approach to living life. I am thankful to have him in my life as my great friend, and I know his contribution to YBLS with his infectious spirit will continue to inspire thousands.

I learned a lot about integrity from my mom too. "An obstacle new business-owners will most likely face at some point is not being taken seriously. You must quickly establish your credibility by convincing the business world of your skills and abilities. Speak with authority. Say what you mean and mean what you say. Once you have proved your credibility, you will quickly notice increased support and more doors of opportunity opening for you," she said.

In and outside of corporate America, people appreciate straight shooters. Honesty and speaking your perspective with authority will take you far.

Keys:

Do your homework when following leaders.

Social media can be an incredible time suck. It seems as if everyone and their brother are going online to promote themselves and establish a following. With this wave of social media gurus, there comes a host of posers who claim to have a huge audience or who buy likes and followers to appear popular. Make sure you invest your time wisely, following people who are genuine, authentic, and heart-centered. With a few clicks of the mouse, you can research people and verify if they are for real, and check out their experience in your field of interest. Check Amazon for books they have written, YouTube for a channel with numerous videos, various podcast apps to see if they have a program with episodes available, and, of course, Google them to see what's being said about them online.

Seek groups that resonate with you and your interests.

In addition to my work with Your Best Life, I am one of the founding members of the large mastermind group, GoBundance, a tribe for healthy, wealthy, and generous men who chose to live epic lives.

Find a group that resonates with you. Offer to spearhead a meeting or organize a gathering to jumpstart your membership. This will ensure you surround yourself with like-minded people who share common interests with you and help you stand out from the crowd and gain the notice of people on the same path as you. Many people like to be involved, but few people like to take charge. Be proactive.

 **Tools:**

- **Leverage OPT** (other people's time) for social media. Many people specialize in this area. Use a social media manager to help manage the minutia, allowing you to devote your valuable social media time in more productive and satisfying ways.

- **Be genuine**. Remember, each of us is unique and can enlighten other's lives, so don't get caught thinking small or being shy when approaching others in networking situations. We all bring gifts to the party of life. Develop the mindset that life itself is an opportunity to network. Help this along by asking yourself questions like, "What am I becoming? Do I like the person I am becoming? Am I happy with what I am getting and giving?" Focus on giving to find the most joy in networking. Doing so will help you develop genuine friends that will last a lifetime.

CHAPTER 7

Constant and Never-Ending Development

Continuous improvement is better than delayed perfection.

Mark Twain

As I crept toward bankruptcy from 2008 to 2012, it felt, for a time, as if everything of value had been taken away from me. But, during this cyclone of diminishing net worth, I learned money and financial success have nothing to do with emotional fulfillment, personal value, or depth of character. 80% of multi-millionaires have gone bankrupt or find themselves in financial despair. While I might have lost money and property, no one could take away my emotional net worth. Thus, I was in decent shape!

Had I not gone through various programs, investing time in education and personal development, I might have spiraled downward and not recovered from such a massive change in my life and financial situation. This is a point I encourage you to reflect upon when deciding how much time and effort to devote to self-development. Far too many people spend a disproportionate time focused on earning money when they'd be better off using some of their time to learn and add value to their knowledge bank because the best investment anyone can make is in themselves.

Net worth rises and falls daily depending on many variables, including the markets, and cannot be controlled. What you can control is how you feel about yourself, the educational inputs you plug into your brain every day, and your sense of curiosity and wonder about things you don't know and in the world around you.

Invest in your education and personal development. Feeding your brain isn't just about gaining knowledge. It increases your confidence and belief in yourself as you expand your experiences and thoughts. These investments are like investing in ultra-safe securities that pay a steadily increasing dividend. Education and personal development always increase in value and will continue to do so for the rest of your life.

The Giving/Self-Development Correlation

Giving back to society and contributing to charities and other worthy causes is a form of self-development I highly encourage you to consider. Giving back to society doesn't have to be a monetary donation. It could be volunteering your time or donating items to organizations that can put them in the hands of people in need.

The magic of giving comes from the intangible value of helping people and what that does for your spirit and well-being. Knowing you make a difference gives you a boost in ways that cannot be bought or obtained otherwise. For me, giving back is a key part of feeling emotionally fulfilled.

I believe if everyone gave a small part of their time and money every year, the world would be vastly improved. The expression, "The more you give, the more you get," represents the reciprocal value of giving. The more you give, the more you receive and can pass along to others. When you give, everyone benefits, including you.

Every year, I spend approximately one month of my

vacation time away from corporate America and my investment businesses, volunteering my time as a trainer for seminars (usually with the Tony Robbins organizations.) Though I'm not donating money out of my pocket, I am away from my businesses for periods of time, so there is still a definite monetary value to the time I invest.

I am constantly learning, growing, inspiring, and giving back, which aligns with my purpose and makes volunteering time well spent. My businesses have continued to prosper over the last several years, and I've added more tools to my knowledge bank.

Some people might prefer to give money to charitable organizations, and this is fantastic. Giving is giving, but I'd suggest you look at ways you can give and learn at the same time.

For many years, I have been involved with various nonprofit charitable organizations. One of the organizations I work with is Child Fund International. I sponsor poverty-stricken children in Ecuador and Mexico by sending money monthly. Last year, I began working with Mission 1:27, an organization that helps orphans in Ethiopia and assists struggling families. My pal, Jeff Butler, heads up this foundation as the chairman. He sees it as his mission to give back to the world.

My good friend, Tim Rhode, heads up the nonprofit 1

Life Fully Lived, which helps supply people of all ages the tools to succeed in life. It is an honor to help contribute to these foundations that give hope and opportunity to others.

There are many opportunities to give back, not just financially. I have friends who volunteer with animal rescue and foster groups. Others give their time to local schools and libraries dedicated to getting books into the hands of children.

Find a cause that fits you. Know the rewards you reap will be worth far more than the time and money you give. Giving and contributing to others offers intangible value and benefits.

My stepfather Steve Diamond's past and present actions and tremendous heart and example have taught me a lot about giving. He is constantly caring for a wide reach of people. Whether he's dealing with close family, extended family, or nonprofits, he always strives to be the giver and not the taker.

Business survival depends on owners and managers who are sensitive to the needs of their clients and employees too. Long gone are the greedy me-me-me decades. Today, men and women in business are in a unique position to use skills that were once viewed as weaknesses but come naturally to so many: nurturing and empathy. Sensitivity of the heart is a strength, not a weakness. Thinking of others is an advantage in business today and is essential to success.

Value your employees. Always give back whenever you can, and you will find success and attract an excellent crew of people to work with. When one has an excellent product and is surrounded by tremendous people, the road to success becomes much easier.

Make sure to take care of the golden goose first (you). The world needs you at 100% and not running half empty. Make personal care and health one of your top priorities. Add personal development to your list of things to do in this area, as health isn't just about what you do for your body. Your soul and brain need care too.

Humility

None of us knows everything. The most educated and experienced person still has areas they must enrich with learning to stay at the top of their game or expand their thoughts into new areas. By practicing humility, when it comes to your knowledge and experience, you remind yourself and others that you don't know it all and haven't seen it all. This is critical for expanding your mind and building relationships with others.

Don't take classes or attend seminars where you are the smartest person in the room. Don't join an easy crowd just because they like you or because you want to fit in. Look for a mix of experiences and opportunities to grow. This will keep you fresh and eager to participate.

Be a small fish in a big pond when you approach learning and growth. Hang out with people who can teach you and show you things in a manner you might never have considered. These people will push you and expand your thinking about what's possible, taking you to the next level in your business and in life.

Remember, you can learn something from everyone you meet no matter who they are, where they're from, or how much or little money they have. Be open to these opportunities. Be humble and look for opportunities everywhere. Some of the best come from an open mind and our everyday interactions with others.

Sharpening Your Winning Edge

Growing up, as one of the smallest kids around, I developed grit and tenacity from such an early age that I felt as if I was born with it. Now, I realize these traits were developed as I matured. What I lacked in size, I made up for in scrappiness and resolve.

Tapping into your gifts and natural talents is one way to give yourself a winning edge. Take a minute to look back at your life's experiences, reframing even the "bad" ones in a way that allows you to see the value they brought to your character. This is a major step to letting go of the past, taking with you only the best parts of you and your experiences.

If you're not sure where to begin, start with what you know and the natural abilities you have before going off half-cocked in ten different directions. Tap into the knowledge of your inner circle before you begin reaching out to everyone in your network. Work methodically from the inside out and take advantage of the many ways to learn in today's world.

With most new endeavors, it pays to start in your own backyard. Even though my life is extremely blessed in many areas, I cannot claim to be 100% where I want to be because this takes time, and the targets are always evolving. Yet, I know with continued investment in myself, applying the principles outlined in this book, I will be there before I know it, and you can be too.

Manage your inputs.

A key factor in developing a winning edge is managing your inputs and sources of information. There are many sources of data and various modes of delivery—watching, listening, and doing. Most of us have a method of learning that works best, so pick sources that support your primary mode of learning, but don't be afraid to try different things to shake things up.

One of the most influential sources of information is people. Learning from another person often gives you all three inputs at the same time, but only if you make a point to choose positive people to hang around with. When you spend time with people who are focused on their goals, who are success-oriented, and refuse to give up, no matter what obstacles they run into, their example and attitude rub off on you. If you choose to hang around people who are constantly frustrated and blame the world for their woes, their energy will find its way into your thinking, even if only temporarily.

Reading books is a fantastic way to improve your life. Books supply nuggets of goodness you can apply to your life and perspectives on things that will move you toward your goals and dreams.

When I was younger, I struggled to read books and had to read them repeatedly to get the point. Then, I'd go buy the CliffsNotes! I went on to become an English major in college, not because I am a glutton for punishment but because I really wanted to improve my communication skills.

Reading becomes easier and more fun when you pick topics that resonate with you and authors who deliver information in ways that hold your interest. Now, I make a point to read more and focus my reading choices on topics I enjoy. Learning is more fun and enjoyable as a result.

Life is short, so do what you love as often as possible. When you must learn topics you don't particularly care about, and it seems like a chore, shift your perspective, and widen the lens to see the bigger picture, then finish the task so you can get back to what you love doing as quickly as possible.

Watching inspirational movies has been a fun way for me to get instant motivation. I don't mind watching underdog, inspirational movies like *Good Will Hunting*, *Rudy*, and *Rocky* over and over. Classic movies can inspire you and fill your head with positive messages when times are tough. Think about movies you've seen that lifted you up or made you think and revisit them.

Perhaps movies are not your thing, and a good song or book might fit the bill instead. Don't hesitate to listen again to that great song or reread that special book as they just may ignite something inside of you in ways nothing else can.

If you're an internet lover, go to YouTube and search for people achieving remarkable things, sometimes against tremendous odds. There are thousands of real people creating videos and short movies that can kickstart you in a positive direction.

Listening to audiobooks and podcasts is another way to work on constant development. By turning your car into a rolling classroom, you can make excellent, productive use of your drive time each day. If you commute to work, this time is probably the largest block of downtime you have during the week. Consider how quickly you could advance on a subject by maximizing this time to your advantage.

I have listened to many classic professional development people like Tony Robbins, Jim Rohn, Zig Ziglar, Les Brown, Jack Canfield, Brian Tracy, and others, over and over. Their messages are timeless, and everyone can benefit from them at any point in their life. These men have lived well-balanced, successful lives doing what they loved to do. I want that too, so I pay attention to people who know what I want to know and have what I want to have.

Listen repeatedly to valuable programs so the wisdom can become part of your subconscious mind. When you find something you really love, share it with your friends and family.

Schooling

When it comes to standardized education, there are certain

requirements set in place to ensure people are given the basics—reading, writing, arithmetic, language, and science. Recently, with the Covid-19 outbreak, more people are exploring homeschooling and private education. Regardless of where children go to school, they need to attend and achieve certain milestones. After high school, it's their choice to continue learning, and they must figure out how they will go about the process. As an adult, you can enroll in continued learning classes or go back to school to earn a higher degree or needed occupational certifications.

What I find interesting is how often I hear kids and adults complaining about having to go to school or about the quality of teachers, facilities, programs, and equipment they have at their disposal. Yet, children in third-world countries who have no schools would give anything to have a fraction of the opportunities we do in the States.

Some people come from a background where they were given a golden ticket at birth and have financial security and a relatively easy life without much effort. Having financial success is important, but it doesn't guarantee emotional fulfillment. Money is a crucial resource that gives us options and flexibility, but it cannot buy emotional success, joy, or inner peace.

A sense of entitlement without production or growth adds up to a lot of nothing. The most successful, happy people earn their keep and work for the things they have in life. The things we own and the services we enjoy have more value when we earn them. If we are given things with no effort on our part, the silver-spoon syndrome, we develop a skewed view of what is important. This circles back to the importance of continuous development and education.

No matter what you have, or where you came from, or how much money you have in the bank, you need to earn self-fulfillment by pushing yourself to explore new things. You must master how to think, not just what to think, while learning the basics in school. The efforts you make in this area will leave you happier, more fulfilled, and equipped with everything necessary to live a peaceful, happy life.

Development During Rough Times

In 2001, during the unfortunate events of September 11th, I was attending my first multiday personal development seminar by Tony Robbins. I met a nice woman from New York during the seminar, before the tragic events unfolded. We shared notes about our desired outcomes for the event, and it was nice to see how open and friendly everyone was from all around the world. Then, tragedy hit. I was shocked and tried my best to console the woman from New York when she confided in me that her soon-to-be fiancé had been killed in the explosion.

Chills raced down my spine when she shared the voicemail he left her before the end came. "Farewell, my love. I love you," he'd said, knowing his chances of survival did not look good.

His voice was much calmer than I would have expected. It was a near miracle his phone call went through as phone lines in New York were jammed. I like to believe that he knew she had no control over his outcome. So, he wanted to make sure she was left with an empowering, loving message since his destiny was someplace else.

There was a tremendous amount of healing and bonding of friendships that happened during this event. It made me open my eyes to a whole new world outside myself. I knew it was my purpose to inspire people as I was inspired, sharing my trials and tribulations with the world. The environment at this event was so open and brutally honest that there was no hiding. It was game on!

After that experience, I was hooked on the personal development field and on improving myself. I attended a lot of Tony Robbins events and started to volunteer at events around the world because I did not have the means to pay for the events at the time. Eventually, as my finances vastly improved, I joined the Tony Robbins leadership track, regularly returning for events. I took part in training programs while continuing my self-development education, becoming master certified in neuro-linguistic programming in 2005. Eventually, I was promoted to trainer within the Robbins organization, and I help at various international events as time allows.

Personal development programs are excellent sources of new ways of thinking and education in areas that directly affect your personal growth. I've attended many. Highlights were Tony Robbins, Steve Linder, Keith Cunningham, Joe Williams, Brendon Burchard, and Rock Thomas.

Find Your Personal Development Tribe

Years ago, when I had been dating my ex-girlfriend off and on for seven years, I discovered she wasn't into personal development. She thought self-development was an American thing, a rah-rah situation with a lot of noise but little value. Her attitude was that you should be strong enough to figure out life for yourself. Despite her opinions, I believed in personal development pursuits and continued pursuing courses and training that worked for me. In hindsight, this difference in thinking was a red flag I ignored at the time.

While it's beneficial to interact with people who have differing viewpoints, your tribe and those closest to you should support your efforts and ultimate goals. Ideally, you should seek out people to share personal development endeavors with who will hold you accountable and cheer you on. My precious wife, Laura, is my biggest fan and is constantly encouraging me to continually learn and grow more. She is an aspiring life and nutrition coach, and I am her biggest fan.

Keys:

Give more than you take.

Develop ways (volunteering, donations, teaching, writing, etc.) to contribute to the world.

Stay consistent and repeat.

Like brushing your teeth, personal development isn't a one-time thing. Even if you do it for five minutes a day, feeding your brain something of value every day is crucial for your success in life.

No excuses

If you are busy, personal development could be a simple commitment to learning something new every day. Learn a new word. Listen to a new podcast. Talk to someone you don't know. Read for five minutes. Whatever it is, take the time. Our brains are meant to continually grow, and if we are not growing, we're dying intellectually. To keep yourself consistent, schedule this learning the way you do everything else on your calendar.

Positive incantations

Recite positive incantations during downtime, whether this is in bed, in the shower, car, bed, or when sitting at red lights. This practice will pay huge dividends by allowing your subconscious mind to readily absorb positive thoughts. Repetition makes your identity stronger.

 **Tools:**

Personal-development organizations – Your Best Life, Tony Robbins, Ml, Gobundance, Brendon Burchard

Audiobooks – Turn your car into an audio library. These are some of my favorite audiobooks:

- *The Traveler's Gift* by Andy Andrews
- *The Four-Hour Workweek* by Tim Ferris
- *Awaken the Giant Within* by Tony Robbins
- *As a Man Thinketh* by James Allen
- *The Seasons of Life* by Jim Rohn
- *Key to Living the Law of Attraction* by Jack Canfield
- T*he 7 Habits of Highly Effective People* by Steven Covey
- *Think and Grow Rich* by Napoleon Hill
- *How to Win Friends and Influence People* by Dale Carnegie
- *High Performance Habits* by Brendon Burchard
- *Developing the Qualities of Success: How to Stay Motivated* by Zig Ziglar

Recommended Reading:

- *The Richest Man in Babylon* by George Samuel Clason
- *Live Your Dreams* by Les Brown
- *Relentless* by Tim Grover
- *Can't Hurt Me* by David Coggins

- *Tribe of Millionaires* by David Osborn, Pat Hiban, Tim Rhode, Mike McCarthy
- *The Front Row Factor* by Jon Vroman
- *The Miracle Morning* by Hal Elrod

CHAPTER 8

Never. Ever. Quit.

Money grows on the tree of persistence.

Japanese Proverb

For most of us, success doesn't come easily, nor should it. If success were too easy, I doubt you would savor or appreciate it when you achieved it. The road to success is paved with bumps, and persistence is the only way over them. But remember that every bump is there to serve you and help you grow. When the climb gets rough, imagine how sweet it will be to stand on top of the mountain, triumphant. Think about how fulfilled you will be looking back at the rough landscape you traveled to get there.

Many professional athletes use focused visualization as part of their training. Imagine the persistence, focus, and consistency it takes to reach the Super Bowl. Persistence isn't just about winning the big game; it must span the entire season. Focusing on the big picture drives the individual players to work together and keep coming back after setbacks, being knocked down, outplayed, scored upon, and making mistakes that put them farther behind in any given moment in each game. Persistence, in this instance, is both an individual and a team mindset. Players at this level do whatever it takes to win, and this work-ethic is reinforced by the head coach and coaching staff in team meetings and practices.

If the team starts to get off track, the coach reminds them of their primary goal by focusing on why it's important and why they deserve to win. Focus acts as a bridge between the bigger picture and the play-by-play within individual games. By focusing on the big goal, the team is energized to do whatever it takes to win the championship, one play at a time.

Here is where consistency is essential. By executing each play as regularly as they rehearsed in practice, the players stand the best chance of winning each game. By winning one game at a time, they have the best chance to reach the championship game and have an opportunity to come out on top. But first, they must always break from the huddle that precedes each play in every game focused on one thing at that moment—the very next play.

Persistence is all about consistent execution at the highest level possible in any given situation. The only way to do this is to apply laser-like focus to your consistent daily efforts. Be clear about what you want, and then pay attention to what you are doing while you are doing it. Like a pro athlete, use a variety of methods to train for success and use visualization as motivation.

Get Real About Your Nature

Most people have a self-defined idea about their nature, their approach to work, and how they do things. Some might say, "I'm type-A" or, "I'm OCD." Others might say, "I'm laid-back," or, "I go with the flow."

How you define yourself has the power to help you by focusing your energy in ways that allow you to get things done because this is how you are and how you do things. These definitions can also limit you by acting as excuses, keeping you in familiar patterns, or holding you back from progress and positive change.

If you believe you are a person who is always late, you

will be late most of the time. You can laugh it off and joke about it to make your excuses more palatable, but you have an issue that affects other people by disrespecting their schedule and the value of their time.

You could tell people you want to climb Mt. Everest, but if you think you're too laid-back to get off the couch and start training, eventually, you will begin to believe your own B.S. and will never see this dream through to fruition. You'll feel the sting of not accomplishing your goal, tempered by the pain that always comes when we make excuses or rely on fallback positions that speak to our nature.

Get real about your nature by closely examining what you genuinely want. What is the value of your goals and dreams? If climbing Mt. Everest is a goal you are passionate about, identify the life-changing value of achieving it. This will get you on the right track and help you find goals worthy of pursuit and effort. The more you understand the value and reasons behind your goals and work to fit them into your true nature, the easier it becomes to avoid the pain of not achieving them.

People are more motivated by avoiding pain (doing nothing) than they are by seeking pleasure (accomplishing something). They might not have figured out what they want, but they know what they don't want. Some people figure out their true calling in life by applying this approach to finding the right career. For example, if you know you don't want to work in an office, you can immediately eliminate many careers. If dealing with sickness makes you want to cry, a career in the health industry is probably out. Use your knowledge of self to your advantage. Use it to cut negatives and illuminate positives, and to motivate yourself to keep going.

Sometimes, when enthusiasm wanes, it helps to focus on the pain of not accomplishing your goals or following your heart. If visualizing success isn't cutting it for you, try visualizing the pain of failure. Amp it up in your mind, and you will stand a greater chance of getting things done if only to avoid the pain of failure.

Remember, though we all battle negative thoughts and should strive to keep them at a minimum, they can be powerful motivators too. When you know the value of your goals and why they are important to you, then magnify the value of the pain of not achieving them, the path of least resistance is less appealing than simply getting back to work and making things happen.

Develop Courage and Tenacity

Courage and tenacity are essential to accomplishing goals and doing things that are new and unfamiliar. Pushing my limits, though I can't deny this is scary, helps build my tenacity muscle, and encourages me to laugh in the face of possible failure.

Fear is inside us all. I'm not one of those people who is completely fearless when it comes to anything new. I evaluate situations and consequences before jumping in with both feet, and I have developed my sense of courage by looking for small ways to be more courageous every day in the workplace, in my personal life, and while playing sports. With every opportunity, I have to push past the fear of trying new things.

Facing the unknown is uncomfortable, but there are few better feelings than digging deep and finding resources to push past presupposed limits and fears.

Learning to be tenacious is like working your muscles with weights a little at a time. The more reps you do, the stronger you become. The stronger you become, the more weight you can lift. Whenever you act despite fear or doubt, you reveal the true potential of who you are and who you can become.

Many people are tenacious in some areas but not in others. Maybe they excel at work but can't seem to bring themselves to be social. If this is you, the next time you are in a social setting where you see someone you would like to get to know, instead of holding back and living with regret, approach them and say something nice or offer a kind gesture. At work, you may wish to participate in meetings more often but are afraid to raise your hand and speak in front of a group. Try doing it once. Sometimes, that's all it takes to break the ice and show yourself that you are not limited by your past behavior or fears.

Exercise your courage muscle in small ways. Random acts of courage help you grow stronger and more confident every day. Massive growth awaits on the other side of being uncomfortable. Work to conquer your fears, and just go for it!

Follow the Leaders

Watching my mom build her business was like attending classes on persistence and courage. She worked extremely hard, for endless hours, to achieve her goals and is still one of the hardest workers I know.

Before my parents' divorce, my parents combined their unique talents, tinkering around on fixer-upper boats. My dad, who is still my go-to person whenever I have a question about fixing anything around the house, worked on the mechanical and maintenance aspects of the boats. Mom was the interior designer. They liked to entertain friends in Chicago, then New York, and, eventually, in the San

Francisco Bay area when my dad was transferred. They loved the water, so the City by the Bay was a perfect fit for them.

They began their business by buying an inexpensive bargain boat and fixing it up. Then, they upgraded to a larger boat that also needed some attention. They used their natural talents to find their way in this new adventure together.

"A natural is a person who has talents, skills, or abilities. If we just do what comes naturally to us, we do it well. If we persist, we can become successful," my mom said, attributing much of her success to her natural traits combined with persistence.

When my parents split up, Mom took her natural talents for interior designing and networking and focused her energy on fixing up a few of our older family boats, ultimately expanding into a fleet of luxury yachts headquartered in one of the most important ports in the world. Along the way, life brimmed with challenges and adventures.

When I was eight years old, before my parent's divorce, my father bought a sixty-foot vessel in Fort Lauderdale. The parents loaded us three children (ages eight, ten, and twelve), a tutor, and a small crew on the boat and cruised—survived is a better word—from Florida, through the

Panama Canal, to the West Coast. On the way, the yacht was extensively damaged during a storm in Cozumel and had to undergo repairs before we could continue the voyage to California. Ultimately, the boat was docked and refurbished behind our house in Tiburon, California, and the yacht charter business was formally launched, with our home serving as company headquarters.

Dad was instrumental in getting the boat certified and licensed, and he hired the captain. Mom cooked in our kitchen with the neighborhood children who stuffed mushrooms and helped her prepare hors d'oeuvres. She recruited neighboring mothers who thought this was a great adventure. Mom took them on cruises as hostesses, bartenders, and galley crew, sometimes using their favorite appetizers to serve the guests.

Mom devoted her energies to marketing and sales, menu design, cooking, and clerical work, and she worked all the charters. You can see why I was, and still am, impressed by all she managed and by her grit and determination to succeed.

The few clients my parents had were happy, and They referred others to us. Soon, my parents bought a second, larger vessel, the Pacific Spirit, which was old, tired, and in need of a makeover but was charming. That led to another two-and-a-half-month trip through the Caribbean and

Panama Canal for the family. This time I got seasick only once.

Once this new boat was refurbished behind our house, the business's office staff almost doubled as the business grew one event at a time.

There were many adventures, but it wasn't all smooth sailing. My parent's difficult divorce was hard for everyone. My mom hung on by her fingernails, trying to keep the business together and—as a single parent—trying to be a good mother and provider. We ate a lot of charter leftovers, but we felt blessed to have food on the table.

"During my bleakest moments, I began to mentally design the perfect charter yacht, something classy and elegant, that could cater to corporate clients' needs, yet be the perfect setting for weddings and other personal celebrations. Had it not been for friends who really believed in me, I would have lost the business. I was turned down for financing by thirteen institutions over a two-year period and had to sell my first charter boat before finding a lender to make my dream yacht a reality," Mom said.

That's all behind her now. The business has grown throughout the years, and Mom is remarkably successful. She attributes much of her success to the people she's worked with along the way. "I always looked for people with natural talents, abilities, and skills, and it paid off enormously. I've always believed that if you provide the best product and best people, the guests will come, and profits will follow, even in recessionary times."

Mom's spirit, vision, and constant persistence contributed greatly to her success too. She continues to inspire me with all she does.

Embrace FEAR (Fun, Embrace, Achieve, Resilience)

We're all fearful at times, regardless of how big and strong or educated or good-looking or powerful we might appear to others. Anyone who tells you otherwise is putting on a front to impress you or is not being real with themselves.

I went through a period of frightening uncertainty due to my epilepsy, about whether I was closing my eyes for the last time on this earth. All the seizures I had occurred in my sleep, including the violent ones when witnesses thought my life was ending. These episodes eventually created a fear of sleep that took all the resources I had to overcome. During this time, I kept my fears to myself because I didn't want anyone to worry about me, especially my family. In hindsight, I probably would have been better off sharing my fear and facing it with the help of loved ones sooner.

Consistently using the fab 4 got me to the other side when times were rough and created a sense of peace within me. I knew there was a reason for me to still be around despite my various close calls. I believe God wanted me to kick it up a notch and share my gifts with others while appreciating them more.

One of the first things I had to do to make that happen was to conquer my fears.

Many acronyms relate to fear. A popular one is "false evidence appearing real." But my favorites are "face everything and rise" and "fun, embrace, achieve, resilience" because of their more positive nature.

Fear = Fun

It's difficult to be scared when you're having fun. Feelings of fear and anxiety are remarkably like those of fun and anticipation. By changing your mindset and telling yourself you will have fun no matter what, you open the door to acceptance, love, and support. Being ready and able to laugh at yourself and make fun of uncertain situations is a powerful choice you can make. I made a conscious decision the day I refused to feel fearful about closing my eyes and going to sleep. I decided I would live a fun, purpose-driven life each day.

If I'm feeling anxious before giving a presentation, I look to the back of the room and imagine fear is a giant Buddha, laughing and smiling, having a grand time. This image is so silly and so fun that I can't help smiling, which connects with people and distracts me from any fear. It changes my focus from me, which is a selfish mindset, to others. People are more forgiving and likely to laugh along with you when you relax and let go of fear. This helps a lot because we almost always feel less fear in a supportive group.

The next time fear strikes you, try thinking of your fear as a great big, jelly-bellied friend. Laugh at him. Laugh with him. Laugh at yourself and the situations you face together. He isn't going anywhere, so why not enjoy your time together and have some fun with your fear?

I remind myself that the experience of public speaking is not about me. It's about the people in the audience. Remember that people in an audience genuinely want you to succeed. They want to be informed and entertained. They're probably happy it's you up there and not them! They are human and know that if not today, someday soon, they will face their own fears.

Don't forget to smile even if you're nervous. People love genuine, happy people. They will remember a fraction of what you tell them, but they will always remember how you made them feel.

Fear = Embrace

I like to embrace that big, smiling Buddha in the back of the room with a big mental hug. You can face your fears by embracing them too. Wrap your arms around them and be thankful for their presence. There is something oddly exhilarating and magical about being grateful for fear. Like in a movie where the monster keeps trying in vain to scare the small child and the child keeps smiling and welcoming him with candy and treats, eventually, the monster gives up and throws his arm around the child, and they become friends. Remember that fear is a gift as, without it, one's growth will be severely limited.

When I'm skiing and about to throw myself over the edge of a cliff on my next jump, I visualize the route, a successful jump, and a flawless landing. I embrace the rush of adrenaline fear brings with it and give thanks to fear for supplying such a positive feeling.

There are many ways of looking at fear—some people give away their power and control, handing it over to fear, while others disarm fear by embracing it and rejoicing in its presence. Embrace all fears and challenges because they are meant to serve us while taking our mindset to the next level.

Fear = Achieve(s)

Get in the habit of imagining the outcomes of your efforts

before you start and reverse engineer the process by beginning with the end in mind. Train your brain to focus on achievement by thinking things through and reinforcing your why. One creates their best with love, hard work, and imagination.

Visualization and imagination allow you to begin feeling the good vibes that come with accomplishment right from the start. These good feelings beat fear almost every time. Focus on what you hope to achieve and imagine being over the finish line and in the winner's circle. It probably feels damn good. The promise of this achievement and the good feelings that will come with it will probably be enough motivation to push you to take the first step. Often, that's all we need to keep moving. For example, in preparation for a large presentation, I visualize—in advance—the smiles, laughs, appreciation, and applause I will receive from the audience after I give an impressive and inspirational talk. This pushes me past any nervousness or fear that trickles in.

Fear = Resilience

You are not always going to succeed your first time up to bat. You may strike out a dozen times before you get your first hit. Fear will be right there with you, smiling and laughing each time you miss and come back to the plate to try again.

What should you do if all else fails, and fear starts to feel like a vise that won't let you move? Be resilient.

To be resilient is to be flexible in your outlook and adaptable in your reaction to events. You don't have to be locked-in to one way of feeling. Anxiousness and nervousness are not permanent states of being. Use your flexibility to escape fear's clutches. Turn your anxiety into an embrace of your jelly-belly friend named fear. Smile at his presence, say thanks for being here for me. Laugh with him and think about how lucky you are to have his support. Then, think about all the times he was there before, and you kept on trucking. Decide to continue your efforts, then just do it. It seems crazy, right? But crazy is often exactly what we need to kick fear's ass.

I don't care!

Another crazy approach to overcoming fear is by declaring, "I don't care!" There is tremendous power in saying these words and in the underlying attitude.

"I don't care." Say it out loud the next time you're battling fear. Feel how liberating it is to have the words roll off your tongue. These words have nothing to do with being careless in your efforts or sloppy in your work ethic when you say them in response to fear.

When you can walk out on the stage of life prepared to give it your best shot and genuinely not care what happens, good things happen. You connect with your audience. They sense your vulnerable humanness and accept you for who you are—one of them. They want you to succeed.

When you can imagine the worst-case scenario and accept that you will live to fight another day no matter what happens, there's nothing left to fear.

Approximately six years ago, I faced down fear on a mountain in Steamboat Springs, Colorado. It was early morning, and the snow conditions were ideal. There were only a few people on the slopes. There had never been a better time to shoot for a scary target—over 80 MPH, which is the world of Olympians when they race. I pushed fear aside and shot down the mountain, going 79.4 mph. Ski patrol gave me a warning, almost pulled my ski ticket for the day, and added me to the blacklist of people to keep an eye on. Still, I'd almost reached my goal, despite my initial fear. I was eager to try again.

Earlier this year, I got my chance. In South Lake Tahoe, the scene was almost the same as it had been in Colorado. The conditions were pristine. It was early, and the snow was slippery-fast. Despite uncertainties about my age and my fear of skiing at a high rate of speed at the ripe age of forty-nine, I still wanted to know how it felt to go the speed of an Olympic downhill skier.

As I took off, I pointed my skis straight down the mountain. Fear rushed through me. My skis chattered as my speed increased. My sole focus was on keeping my skis in front and staying as low as possible. It felt like I was in a wind tunnel, going faster and faster. Tall, majestic pine trees lined up to form a passageway about fifty feet across that seemed to narrow as my speed increased.

Before heading down the slope, I had visualized laying down a perfect ski line, hauling butt in my mind. Just like in my vision, as I raced down the mountainside, the wind rushed over my helmet, arms, and legs. I focused on the fun and embraced my fear when it came, and I focused on what I wanted to achieve, knowing I'd put in the work to make it happen and was okay with the idea of failing. I did not think of catching an edge and falling as that would have probably been the end of it for me. I was solely in a zone and zoomed toward the bottom of the hill without turning. Little butterflies circled around my stomach, and I entered a euphoric state. When I ended my run, I pulled my phone out of my pocket and checked my skiing app, blown away with a sense of accomplishment when I saw my final speed—91.6 mph! The locals told me this was a record at this resort, which had hosted several Olympic gold-medalist skiers. It was pleasing to know someone pushing fifty could still hope to inspire the younger generation.

Naysayers and Negative Influences

A major obstacle in our quest for accomplishment and a frequent cause of worry about trying something new are naysayers and negative people, especially in today's social-media-obsessed world. Much of the negativity and judgments formed there are made without knowing the person on the other side of the screen. With little backstory, people can decide they don't like what someone else said, or how they look, or what they're doing, so they tear into their efforts to do something positive or achieve success publicly.

These naysayers who type before they think are usually in desperate need of an audience and are seeking attention for themselves. Their cowardly behavior is a mask for some internal weakness or shortcoming they are trying to cover up or deflect attention away from.

If you have something critical to say about someone online, I hope you send them a private message and talk to them directly instead of posting something negative or hurtful in a public forum. Hopefully, your opinion and criticism would be formed after getting to know all sides of a story, not some knee-jerk reaction to a single post or statement someone else makes.

When you are a target of negative feedback, in person or online, shield yourself by first understanding that you are like a magician able to control the magic, wield your wand, and cast your spell any way you choose. Step back and examine what you are trying to accomplish and be clear about your intentions. Decide to address the negative person from a place of understanding and be ready to move on if they insist on doubting your ability or continue to try and tear you down. Or ignore them. Cast your magic elsewhere. We all have the superpower to decide what things mean to us.

Remember, too, that the opinions of others are thoughts, not facts. Thoughts need not control you or shake your faith in yourself and your goals. As Henry Ford said after inventing the automobile, "If I had asked people what they wanted, they would have said faster horses."

Before I sat down to write this book, I spent time examining what I hoped to accomplish. Luckily, I didn't have to face naysayers other than ones that came from within myself in the form of fear. I overcame the struggle that came with doing something new and scary by examining my dedication to helping people and building a more positive world. I accepted that I would not reach everyone in the world with my message and framed a version of success that worked for me. I accepted that some people might not like me or my book. I accepted that reality upfront, believing that if even one person's life improves because of my efforts, I will have made a difference. Would I love this book to become a *New York Times* bestseller? Of course I would, but this doesn't have to happen for me to feel great about making the choice to write a book. Once I started, and as the process unfolded, my confidence and self-esteem grew.

Knowing your intentions are good and that you are acting in positive ways will give you the strength to deal with negativity from any source. Build on your positive beliefs about what you are doing. Know that the best thing you can do for the world is to be your most genuine, authentic self. People will feel your positive energy and connect with you deeper.

You owe it to the world to form connections, so build your best tribe. When you are surrounded by supportive people and believe in yourself, it's like wearing a suit of armor that protects you from the naysayers and critics of the world.

Changing Course or Giving Up

There comes a point in most new ventures where you feel

things are not working and you want to give up. You run into a roadblock or face a monumental challenge. After several attempts to get past it or around it, you remain stuck. What do you do? Do you give up? Do you change your goal, so it's easier to achieve? Before giving up, ask yourself these questions:

1. Have my needs changed?
2. Has my desire changed?
3. Am I changing my goals to satisfy my ego?

Giving up or changing your goals when you run into obstacles is a poor habit I don't recommend, primarily because while giving up might provide short-term satisfaction and feel good temporarily, it won't serve you in the long run. If you spent time visualizing your dream and set a goal based on what life would be like and how you'd feel when you accomplished your goal, giving up teaches you it's okay to settle for less. Next comes rationalizing, followed by denial. This nasty cycle won't get you anywhere.

Winners stick to their guns and are persistent about achieving their goals once they've been set. When challenges arise, they make repeated attempts to overcome them, trying novel approaches in the process. After a period with no success, instead of giving up, they step back and reevaluate.

They seek new input from people who can help, and they research to find new ideas. With persistence and resilience, they keep moving forward.

If it turns out your needs have changed, or your desire has genuinely diminished, then you need to assess the value of continuing to pursue a goal that's unnecessary or won't serve you even if you were to follow it through to the end. Let's say your goal was to buy a new car for commuting an hour each way to your job. Then, you are laid off and find a new job working from home. Your needs have changed, and your goals need to change accordingly. It happens. Buying a scooter might be a better goal for you now.

It's important to be honest with yourself when you run into obstacles on the road to success and find yourself wanting to quit. Be careful not to change gears midway just because it's easier. You'll know deep down if this is what's happening. Be aware of your patterns of behavior. What's your track record like when the going gets tough? Only you know for sure.

Putting in the Work and Sticking with It

Getting things done and achieving success requires going the extra mile and putting in a little extra effort. To do this, you need to make a major decision and ask yourself, "Am I going to do only what's required, or am I going to be a star?"

Don't get me wrong, doing what's required can put you well in front of the masses who don't even get that far. There's nothing wrong with getting the job done consistently. If you're a golfer, shooting par (getting the ball in the hole in exactly the number of strokes required for that hole) is fine. If you want to become a pro golfer or the best one on your course, you'll need to practice consistently to begin shooting birdies (one stroke less than the number required for a hole) and eagles (two strokes less).

The difference between good and great is often a shorter distance than people realize, but getting there takes considerable effort, practice, and consistency.

Maybe golf isn't your thing. Look for areas of your life you'd like to improve and set goals to help yourself become a star. Narrow down the steps you'll take until the extra mile becomes more like going one or two feet farther.

In every endeavor, you can consistently improve your results with minimal effort. Adopt a "one extra" or "one more" attitude with your efforts across the board. If you are exercising and shooting for ten sit-ups, do eleven. If you are writing and your goal is to write for thirty minutes, make it thirty-one. Once you are in motion, adding one more is easy. Each time you push yourself to do a little more, you grow stronger. Turn this practice into a game to make it a habit.

From Resistance to Acceptance

Good things will happen if you stay the course, are disciplined, and honor your principles by being genuine and authentic. Set goals, review them, and work smartly, following your plan.

Your patience will be tested along the way. Answers do not come in our time; they come in God's time. Remember, everything that happens is there to serve us. Having our patience tested develops character and resilience as we move forward on our journey. You may lose a few battles, but you will win the war if you are motivated and you commit to staying the course.

Have you ever run across a person who is not motivated to do anything? This affliction is typically reserved for teenagers, though I find it in adults too. The approach I take to shift non-motivated people out of this place is to ask questions that get them thinking. "What juices you? What inspires you? What do you want in life? What's important to you?" If your motivation wanes, ask yourself these questions and dig a little deeper.

If you are trying to help someone else over this hump, it's important to approach them with an attitude of gratitude and humility. Establish rapport and ask quality questions, which will help you get to know them more. I would highly suggest not coming from another perspective and asking directly, "Why aren't you motivated? What's your problem?" Avoid preaching to them. This will only put them on the defensive. Instead, ask if they would take a walk with you or go grab some coffee together. Let them know you are seeking understanding. Let them do you a favor by giving you their time instead of the other way around.

Try asking, "How did you figure out your purpose in life?" Quality questions can help people process their feelings and emotions while providing you with the necessary leverage and feedback to support them through the challenges they are experiencing. Let them take charge of the conversation and help you. In doing so, they will remind themselves of what motivates and inspires them. Hearing themselves say these things out loud can help them get moving in the right direction. They'll find their way to their own answers as you pry open their resistance with your questions.

Remember, we are all driven to satisfy our needs. At the most basic level, we need water, food, shelter, and to feel safe and secure. Without these basics, it's difficult to move up the scale to more advanced needs like love, acceptance, connection with others, opportunities to grow spiritually and intellectually, and contributing to the world by making your mark and developing your legacy. Uncover which needs are the drivers for people, and zero-in on ways to help them see opportunities to grow in those areas. Do the same for yourself.

Spark Persistence with a Higher Purpose

Ask yourself the same types of questions—what gets me fired-up, what's most important to me right now, and who inspires me? To find your higher purpose and a deeper meaning in your life, you must ask better questions, ones that are open-ended and make you think. The reason this can seem so difficult is that it requires effort and energy. It's challenging work. Focus on the rewards of knowing your truth and how this knowledge will feel.

Jack Ma, the founder of Alibaba, grew up in communist China. He started from nothing and became one of the world's richest people. When he started out, rejection was his middle name. Jack was constantly rejected from almost every opportunity he applied for as a young man. He persevered and found the challenges were all blessings in disguise that built his character. Now, he devotes his life to philanthropy, inspiring others with his persistence and leadership. He is still humble and low-key. I could write a book about him; he's achieved so much. For more inspiration, Google him and read about his journey and how far persistence has taken him.

When I joined the team at McKesson, I decided I wanted to earn the title of National Rookie Salesperson of the Year. I was clear about my intention and visualized what it would feel like when I achieved the honor. I was up against many talented representatives across the United States, including Jeff Butler from Seattle. He and I formed a close bond that continues to this day. Our friendly rivalry propelled me to work hard and stay focused.

My pal, John Sullivan, from the Chicago area, who is also a daily inspiration for me as one of the best McKesson account executives, had won the year before. At the awards banquet, all the candidates waited during the award presentation, not knowing whose name would be called. I still remember the thrill of hearing my name, going up on stage in front of my peers to accept the award, filled with pride that I'd achieved my goal. Jeff and I continue to push each other to greater and greater heights, including many President's Club honors and recognition for continuing to raise the bar.

Over the years, while my persistence has never wavered, I've learned to work smarter. When I first began my career in sales, I spent much more time on the road, spinning my wheels by working hard, calling on any medical office that had a pulse or open sign. Now, I work a few days a week from home and spend more of my time supporting fewer, larger clients instead of chasing high quantities of smaller clients. Clients and bigger opportunities call my name now, while, before, I begged for any opportunity to just get prospects to fill out a credit application.

When I was younger, I had the benefit of youthful energy on my side. I often worked by putting my head down and plowing ahead. As I matured, I realized that my time and energy should be focused on the big fish who produce the sales and pay the lion's share of my bills. Figuring out where your greatest rewards come from and focusing your time and energy in that direction is the key to working smart.

Keys:

- Live as if you are living your last day on earth.
- Know the universe (or God) has a plan for you.
- Don't let labels hold you back.

Tools:

Consistency

People often overestimate what they can do in one year and underestimate what they can do in five years. Doing one thing consistently, in the right state of mind, allows you to conquer anything and achieve what you want.

If someone wants to learn a foreign language, they should not try learning four others at the same time. Often, people take on too many things, leading to overwhelm and frustration, which results in not finishing anything. Instead, focus on one thing at a time. Obstacles will still come; however, they will be easier to conquer, and there will be fewer of them. By having the right mindset, conquering one obstacle at a time, your confidence will rise, and so will your resistance.

Try to drop multitasking from your life for one day. Set your tasks and schedule in advance so you know you are on the right track. Every time you switch gears, check yourself, making sure you focus on one thing at a time. If Facebook calls, ignore it until your set-in-advance time, then focus on it alone. See how it feels to come up with a structure that encourages maximum consistency during your day.

CHAPTER 9

Work/Life Balance

You can have it all. You just can't have it all at once.

Oprah Winfrey

When I was younger, my priorities were out of whack. I focused my time and energy on work from sunup to sundown, often working late into the evening. If there was any time left over, I scrambled to take care of issues in my personal life. I almost lost my life a few times because of stress and lack of rest.

My old way of doing things was to set unrealistic and not

very well-thought-out goals for myself, then work day and night, seven days a week, trying to achieve them. I rarely turned off my phone or office technology, constantly scrambling to address new, added demands on my time the instant they appeared. I operated from a scarcity mentality that said, "I must do this now or else."

Make Your Best Life Your Best Habit.

Many people feel obligated to take care of other people's needs first, feeling that being the head of a family or household means they must be the provider at whatever cost. They constantly work, even during the evening and on weekends, checking emails, and doing one more thing, one more thing. The irony of working in this manner is that the family they are working so hard to provide for is missing the key ingredients they desire the most, their loved one's time and undivided attention.

I broke out of this deadly cycle by taking a step back and taking an honest look at what I was doing and where I was underperforming. Then, I looked at the order of my values and what I held closest to my heart. I started placing my family, God, and my health at the top of my mind each week instead of the needs and demands of others. I started scheduling my time and sticking to my schedule, stopping work when I said I would stop. These changes helped me take better care of myself and feel stronger and healthier, mentally and physically.

Be the Engineer

We all must earn a living, so it can be difficult not to make our jobs our focus in life. One way to look at finances and cash flow is as if money is a train that arrives on a regular schedule, carrying the resources you need to operate your life. Think of yourself as the engineer who drives the train. By keeping your life train running smoothly and on schedule, you can build your business and take care of your basic needs.

Though money shouldn't be your sole focus or motivation for work, it is a necessary resource for survival. Part of the necessity of working or building a business is to pay your bills and provide opportunities for you and your family. Keeping the money train running is important and should be one of the factors in your planning and goal setting. As Beatrice Kaufman says, "I've been rich, and I've been poor. Rich is better!"

Remember, even the most loaded money train must stop for fuel, maintenance, cleaning, and refurbishments to avoid a total breakdown and the junkyard.

Faith and spirituality are important too and can be viewed as another car on your life train. Regardless of what doctrine or spiritual path you follow, it's important to get behind your choice consistently.

I give a lot of credit to my dad, who made sure our faith in God was strong. He was always consistent with his Catholic faith, attending church regularly. This consistency inspired my own practice of attending services regularly. To this day, Dad calls to test me by asking what the weekly sermon or talk at mass was about.

When I was a boy, my dad also encouraged me to get involved in sports, primarily baseball and soccer, to foster my belief in myself.

Before becoming one of the coaches, Dad attended my games regularly along with my grandfather on Mom's side, who was a great athlete in his own right. Grandpa was a world-class sprinter and was set to take part in the 1936 Berlin Olympic games versus the famous Jesse Owens before an ankle injury sidelined him a month before the games started. This setback magnified Grandpa's support for my efforts, and my mom echoed his belief and encouragement, especially during the dark times when I was cut a half-dozen times from various teams in high school. "Papa," as my grandfather was nicknamed, was perhaps my greatest fan. He always cheered me on. He was not the biggest guy around either, so his support and stories also offered invaluable inspiration.

Family has always been important to me, but over the years, some of my priorities and perspectives have changed. Today, I center my time and efforts around my family, placing them at the top of my priority list, along with my faith in God and my good health. This doesn't mean my business suffers. It means I am more efficient, scheduling time around these key areas of my life—faith, family, health, and business.

I owe much of this to Laura, the love of my life, and to the recent addition of our first child, Mila. It's amazing what happens when you take the focus off yourself and have other people depending on you.

I was lucky to grow up with parents who recognized the importance of work/life balance, even back when no one was talking about it. Balance is a challenge to business-ownership, and it affects every entrepreneur. Daily, we are called upon to use our abilities to juggle careers, family, and outside interests. Too many times, we throw ourselves into business, forgetting to take care of our personal lives, and our health suffers. There is an urgent need for more well-balanced lives today. To have that, sometimes, we must learn to work smarter and to schedule a few moments for ourselves consistently.

Despite making changes to support my top priorities, my business ventures have grown and are thriving. Instead of scrambling in ten different directions all the time, fighting one fire after another, I work smarter by focusing on the highest payoff activities and top clients first. I have delegated routine responsibilities to other members of my teams, and I strategically go out and find new business only on certain days of the week during the month. I'm no less busy, though I feel more peaceful, grounded, and balanced each day.

The Magic of Scheduling

At the beginning of each year and every quarter, I plan vacation time and get it on the calendar. I do this upfront because I realize the value of taking time off to rejuvenate and unplug from the hustle-bustle of daily life. It's easy to get caught up in the minutiae that leads to burnout. Planning a vacation during each season (winter, spring, summer, and fall) is important for unwinding, and I encourage people to do the same even if they only take a quick three-day weekend away. My approach is to take time off at the beginning of the month, so I can relax and know I have time to adjust my business when I get back if necessary.

It is important to note that everyone needs to rejuvenate

as you cannot serve or be your best if you are running on a half-empty tank or your mind is shot. Bottom line—take time off, and your productivity will rise due to an increase in focus and energy.

I also schedule my time for the upcoming week over the weekend, so I am ready to hit the ground running on Monday morning. This is a habit worth developing because it provides you with focus, energy, and a powerful sense of knowing what you will be doing when it's time to get down to business. Knowing you have your week planned also allows you to relax and focus on your family time without feeling distracted and unsettled.

Are Your Habits Serving You or Are You Serving Your Habits?

Many of my past poor habits had a direct impact on my health and well-being. It's easy to put off eating right, going to the gym, and getting enough rest because the results of bad habits are not immediate. The human body is resilient and can take a ton of abuse. We can slack off in these areas and get by, drinking too much coffee, eating junk food, taking drugs to keep us awake, and taking drugs to put us to sleep. If you don't put gas in your car, you feel the pain immediately when you run out of gas and become stranded.

Unlike your car, your body can keep going well beyond E on the gas gauge. Eventually, you may wake up on the floor in a daze with flashlights in your eyes and people shouting, "Wake up!" and reassuring you that the gates of heaven are not calling your name! But hopefully, it won't have to come to this for you to realize the importance of putting your health at the top of your to-do list.

When it comes to finances, developing healthy habits could require you to change your paradigm or your perspective. You might need to grab your calculator from time to time and run some numbers. For example, if you stop at Starbucks or your favorite coffee house for coffee every morning and spend five dollars, that's twenty-five dollars a week. This may seem reasonable to you. Starbucks coffee is faster and tastes better, right? When you annualize the numbers, it turns out you spend over twelve-hundred dollars a year on coffee! If you go out for lunch every day and spend ten dollars on average, there's another twenty-four hundred dollars you're spending without thought.

If you're carrying a bunch of credit card debt and paying only the minimum payments, the examples above cost you even more because of interest.

Let's say you're saving money for a family vacation. Would thirty-six hundred dollars make a difference? A can or two of premium coffee at home will last you an entire month and costs a heck of a lot less than Starbucks. Making your own lunch or bringing leftovers from dinners you prepare during the week will save you a bunch. Does this take a little extra effort? Sure; however, these minor changes add up. For many people, these monetary checks on your budget may not be necessary, but they certainly were for me when I was first getting started.

Wherever you are in life, managing millions or just starting out, fiscal management and responsibility are important. Wake up ten minutes earlier or prepare your coffeemaker the night before. Make your lunch while you are cleaning up after dinner the night before or in the morning when you get up a few minutes early. Think about minor changes you can make to have big impacts on your bottom line and health.

This is a good time to revisit your notebook and jot down some ideas about how you could save time and money to free up both for a better sense of balance overall in your life.

Create Your Best-Life Habits

Asking simple questions is a terrific way to develop positive habits and figure out what your best life looks like. "Is my daily Starbucks coffee habit or lunchtime eating-out ritual getting me closer to my financial goals? Is my habit of sleeping until noon helping me build my business? Are my daily habits bringing me closer to my vision? Is working all the time helping me have a happy marriage or be a good father?"

Examine your current habits and ask revealing questions. Run some numbers and annualize the results. If you don't have a budget, then start one. It is extremely hard to start saving for investments or a rainy-day if you don't know your numbers. Be honest and real with yourself about the answers.

If you are alarmed by the results of your self-survey and see a disparity between your current habits and your goals, make some simple changes. Get up earlier or block out time in the evening to read or study. Spend a few minutes at the end of your workday or week to schedule your time for the following day or week. Put this scheduling time on your calendar to account for it regularly. Schedule time for fitness activities or combine them with your family time, going for walks or riding bikes together. Plan your meals in advance and stick to a list when buying groceries.

I enjoy peace and serenity in my life because I feel in balance in areas of life that are most important to me. I love sharing this goodness with other people, helping them build the life of their dreams too with freedom and options, financial independence, travel time and adventures, family time, and giving back to the world.

My life is full of joy on many levels. I look back with gratitude for all the blessings I've had. I look at my wife and family, and I feel lucky to have so much love surrounding me. I feel it in my heart and soul. Love is at the center of my purpose in this world. Sharing it with others doesn't deplete my supply; it magnifies it even more. I've moved into a stage of my business life where I'm able to share my experience on a higher level with people who need help growing their businesses or who are figuring out their careers. I help them with strategies to balance their work, family, and personal pursuits, and I am grateful to be able to do so.

Reward Yourself

Many people are too hard on themselves when things go wrong. They are critical of their own performance and do not treat themselves in loving ways. Their self-talk is largely negative, and much of what they say comes across that way. What's interesting is that these same people are often generous with their praise for others, giving compliments and positive reinforcement easily.

Finding fault and being critical of ourselves is a habit that forms over time. We make a mistake, then feel foolish because we're concerned about what other people might think. This behavior usually stems from seeking approval as a child and carries forward into our lives as adults.

Life works better when we develop ways to measure our performance by comparing our results only against our earlier efforts. Often, this new behavior requires a simple shift we can easily make. If being self-critical is a habit, then the good news is being self-confident is also a habit, easily formed with practice.

The more you talk to yourself in positive and encouraging ways, the better you will feel. Even when your results aren't perfect, your efforts alone are always worthy of note. Give yourself a verbal pat on the back after you complete each step in any process or toward any goal. If you are working on your cooking skills, complement your success when you find a recipe that excites you. Remind yourself you are a master of getting the ingredients and cooking tools laid out. Reward yourself and family members with a sample as they cruise through the kitchen, drawn in by the enticing aromas. Make a toast before dinner to the goodness of a home-cooked meal. Be grateful that you have food on the table and a kitchen to prepare it in. Revel in the joy of putting away the leftovers, knowing you will have food available in the coming days when you might not have as much time to cook. Every step you take is an opportunity to be thankful for your own greatness, regardless of how successful the dish was on your first attempt.

Take the time to notice the moments and thoughts that make up our lives. Consciously do so, and it becomes second nature.

Reward yourself often too. The pleasure we feel, making each moment positive, rewarding ourselves for our hard work and good habits does not have to involve spending a lot of money. Whatever you do, and I suggest you reward yourself often, make sure your chosen rewards have a significant emotional value to you. Look for rewards that make you feel good. This could be a relaxing, candlelit bath, a walk with your dog, an early-morning bike ride, a cup of coffee on the deck, an afternoon nap on a lazy Sunday afternoon. Sometimes, a shift in perspective is all that's needed to bring yourself pleasure and a sense of reward. Look with greater appreciation at some of the simple things in life you enjoy. Assign a higher value to them in your mind.

Some rewards might require more planning and investment. Reward yourself on occasion with a night out or by buying something meaningful to you. Set aside a certain amount every month for this type of thing because you deserve it and are worth it. The amount you put aside in this fun bucket is not significant; it is the consistent habit and repetition of taking care of yourself that is.

If you are unable to take long vacations, try taking several smaller getaways. Short road trips are one of my favorites because being in the car is exhilarating, it's spontaneous, and it opens a world of adventure as you travel roads you've never gone down before. You don't have to go far or break the budget either. Try spending a night at a hotel not too far away for a change of scenery. Visit friends or family and spend a day or two with them. Go camping.

Get the picture? Make yourself a top priority when it comes to compliments, encouragement, and regular rewards.

The dark side of not taking care of yourself with positive self-talk, habits, and rewards appears in the form of stress, health issues, and irritability. Soon, you feel rundown and depressed, losing enthusiasm for your goals and dreams. When this happens, life can feel like a perpetual negative spiral that is difficult to stop.

When I was in college and began having seizures, I chalked them up to stress, lack of sleep, a busy student-athlete schedule, and poor habits. I was young and invincible, so I figured they would pass. When doctors began to discuss other possibilities like types of epilepsy, they got my attention. Before I knew it, I had to take medication before bed every night and deal with the realization that I might be fallible. Later, when the periodic seizures became much worse, I was forced to recognize the wake-up calls I was receiving from the man upstairs. Apparently, I hadn't received his urgent messages, so the knocks on the door became much louder. God probably wondered if I had a walnut for a brain!

The human body is resilient, but when you combine that resilience with old thinking, stubbornness, and ego, you quickly find that your body isn't infallible. It took multiple seizures of increasing intensity to finally tear my focus away from my pursuit of the golden ring and the almighty dollar and rededicate my life, so it was much more in balance.

I now realize the golden ring will always be there, but its attainment should not come at the expense of your family or your health. I didn't go about reaching for the ring smartly when I was younger. When I learned how to work smarter and more efficiently while living in balance and continuously learning through the world of personal development, my results shot through the roof. This was despite working fewer hours than when I had my stress-induced seizures.

Before, I was in a relationship that, in hindsight, was an obvious mismatch. Yet, I continued to funnel energy and resources into it, trying to make it work. I should have cut and run much sooner because we grew apart, and the relationship did not serve either of us.

My involvement in the real estate business, which needed my attention during this same period, further compounded my problems. Instead of selling off several properties in various States when they rose in value and investing close to my home, greed and stupidity stepped in and kept me hanging out for more. I can say that now, with a smile on my face. But none of my troubles felt like a picnic at the time.

Yes, I made some stupid decisions that nearly cost me my life, but with the mistakes came wonderful clarity. Not everyone is so lucky.

Finding out I had a form of epilepsy was a blow to my ego and identity at first. I'd felt young and invincible up to that point. Suddenly, I had a new label and a new sense of my mortality and human body. Looking around at my life, I also had many habits to change all at once, a daunting prospect. My ego and identity had a vise grip on my behavior and had formed bad habits I didn't see until it was almost too late. It took a decade of repeated events and signs from above to finally wake me up and spur me to action.

Since then, I've embraced the power of incremental changes. Mine started with small things like slowing down to enjoy the small pleasures in life, giving myself regular rewards, focusing on positive self-talk and self-worth, and becoming conscious of patterns of behavior that were not serving me.

I didn't get married until I was in my mid-forties or become a father until my late forties. Both factors have changed my life in such positive ways, reinforcing the importance of getting outside my own head and focusing on people and things outside myself. My family is the best reward ever.

Relaxing and Still Applying Success Principles

I live about thirty minutes outside of San Francisco, up in the hills, in a park-like setting surrounded by tall redwood and pine trees. The mountain air is exhilarating and allows me to take a few minutes to go for a walk each day or sit outside and breathe in the beauty of my surroundings. Even in short bursts, these small, relaxing moments fuel my other efforts and ground me.

I love to ski, and when the ski season is over, I play golf. When I was younger, I used to think golf was a boring, slow game. Now, I appreciate the game on several fronts—the necessary strategy (similar to business strategy), the skill required, the sense of peace from being outdoors, and the potential for building relationships and doing business while playing a round. A lot of business takes place on the golf course in a laid-back, scenic atmosphere.

When my daughter Mila gets a little older, Laura and I plan to get back into going to the health club more regularly. I am committed to running my first Ironman in the next twelve months. Working out at a gym helps me improve all three Ironman elements (running, swimming, and biking).

The preparation and training process is a big part of my motivation. I don't expect to win or break any records. The fun is in the challenge of preparing for and simply finishing this endurance event. Completing an Ironman is my goal, not winning. I might even do them on an ongoing basis. You never know, and that's a fun place to be. Possibilities!

None of these activities take all my time. All of them are important enough for me to work them into my schedule along with business pursuits, self-development, family and friends, and volunteering. I find the time because I plan it that way. I've set my goals, looked in my heart, and decided these things matter to me.

If you tend to neglect relaxation or put off things that give you pleasure in life because you are too busy or feel you must work all the time, think again. No one must live that way.

Taking Care of Your Body and Your Heart

In addition to feeding your mind healthy, positive information, make a habit of feeding your body healthy, nutritious foods and drinking plenty of water. Treat your body as a high-performance engine and feed it high-quality fuel. Spend a few minutes each day stretching and limbering up your body. It's amazing how much better you will feel when you loosen up your muscles and limber up your joints.

I also recommend practicing yoga. It will complement your daily stretching and provide an opportunity to clear your mind and set your intentions for the day. The mental aspect of yoga is one of the most powerful parts of the practice. If you have ever tried to quiet your mind and think of nothing, you know it's a challenge. We're always thinking, and our mind is always distracting us with one random thought after another. Yoga helps you calm your mind, directing your focus to your breathing. In some ways, it can be like meditation and exercise rolled into one.

There are many yoga programs you can watch online or with apps for your phone. You can also join a class at a yoga studio or gym. Pick programs that resonate with you and grab your attention. Some are faster, meant to break a sweat. Others focus on calm and relaxation, while others target specific areas of the body that might require some healing and gentle care. I find some yoga programs to be a little boring as they repeat the same poses over and over, so I found ones that focus more on mental practice. These seem to work better for me. Find one that works for you. You can find the time if you genuinely want to. Hard-pressed for *any* time? Well, some practices are as short as five minutes.

Take care of your heart too, by practicing gratitude daily, reflecting on all the wonders of the world you live in and all the goodness surrounding you. This acts like a tonic for your body and soul, helping you stay centered and positive. When you're feeling lazy about walking to the kitchen and filling a glass of ice-cold, filtered water, think about people in the world who wake up and walk miles in the dust and heat, with no shoes on, to get water to drink that might not even be clean.

Ask yourself, throughout the day, what you are grateful for right in the moment. We often focus on what we don't have instead of appreciating with full gratitude what we do have in our lives. Make a practice of reviewing and repeating these things when you first wake up and before you go to sleep at night. Pull your partner close to you and let them know how much you appreciate them for being a part of your life. Be thankful for your bed while you're at it.

Finding Inspiration Around You

We're all exposed to examples of people living their best

lives. We grow up learning about positive people who have achieved remarkable things. But sometimes, the best, most accessible, and relatable role-models are in your circle of influence.

Sam Wegert has become a close friend of mine even though I am more than twenty years his elder. He is the most impressive, all-around man that I know under thirty years old. Full of wisdom well beyond his years, Sam is an extraordinarily successful entrepreneur and inspirational person who owns Up Level Martial Arts schools. His multi-state schools train people of all ages in martial arts, teaching them how to be black belts in life. He is a leader whose students exemplify respect, passion, discipline, integrity, and honor.

My sister Danielle O'Doherty is one of the most inspirational people I know. In 2009, she was diagnosed with the same form of pancreatic cancer Steve Jobs had. Yet, she inspires countless people with her bright attitude, infectious energy, and actions. She is the ringleader of a large extended family and does not show one sign of slowing down. A tremendous wife and fabulous mother of three children, Danielle leads by example and is a model for how one should lead one's life in the face of adversity. Danielle is going strong, and there is no doubt in my mind that she will beat cancer. My sister is a shining example of the joy that comes from living life on your terms.

Chuck Hogan, whom I mentioned earlier, has a tremendous heart. He is always seeking to help others. I admire his complete character as a person and the way he manages his career, relationships, and work/ life balance. His example is exemplary.

I met Chuck in 2001 or 2002 when we were getting into the personal development arena. We became perpetual roommates whenever possible at Tony Robbins or Keith Cunningham seminars, where we volunteered and rose through the ranks to become senior leaders. We shared the belief that God had put us on this earth to learn, grow, and serve others at our highest capacity. We were equally committed to volunteering at least a month every year because contributing to the success of others and giving back were key values for us both.

When we eventually became trainers, Chuck stepped up his game by donating more of his time to training others in self-development. He became a head trainer for Global Youth Leadership Summit, a non-profit, personal development seminar that lasts a week a year. Chuck volunteers over two months of his year to others and has become a highly sought-after peak-performance strategist.

New to fatherhood, I frequently ask Chuck for tips on how he balances his important career in corporate America with his role as a trainer for individuals and businesses and still manages to volunteer and spend ample time with his family and enjoy downtime for himself. Though I consider myself rather skilled with my work/life balance and multi-tasking, I have not mastered this at Chuck's level, but he's inspiring me every day, and I know I will get there.

My wife Laura is another person I look to for inspiration in life. She opened my eyes to many new things and increased my commitment to achieving an even higher level of work/life balance.

Meeting her was a magical experience. We met online in 2012 when Laura lived in Texas, and I was fresh off a clean start after my bankruptcy. Five months into our friendship, we finally met in person. I knew she was the one almost from the beginning, and I feel so blessed to have met such a beautiful soul. Laura is the most genuine and loving person I've ever come across. She's gentle and caring, a wonderful mother, and connects with me on so many levels.

After Laura settled in with me in 2014, she wanted to go back home to visit her family in Mexico, where she's originally from. She'd been living in Corpus Christi, Texas, on a ten-year tourist visa, going back every three months to Tampico, Mexico, where her family lived. This journey, a seven-hour bus ride, satisfied the requirement of getting her visa stamped regularly. Laura had been doing this for many years and had probably made the crossing over thirty times. The customs office always stamped her for six months during her trips even though her travels were more like every three to four months, so there was never an issue of her overstaying the allotted time on her visa. Until there was.

When Laura went on a trip to Mexico to visit family after moving with me to California, she tried to return to America, and the U.S. Customs Border Control wouldn't let her back in. They said she had overstayed her time in the United States by three weeks. Stunned after seeing her visa, Laura realized the last stamp she'd received was for three months, not the customary six she had received for years. Her latest trip had taken place right around the three-month mark, and her return was past the deadline. Laura was technically deported.

Our relationship had been getting serious, so I hired an immigration attorney to begin what turned into an excursion through a jungle of red tape. It took a year of battling back and forth and a letter to the head of Homeland Security to get Laura cleared to return to the United States. Before we finally passed this hurdle, I grew impatient with all the red tape procedures and the perpetual waiting period. So, I sent Laura a ticket to meet me in Ecuador. From there, we went to Lima, Peru, then Machu Picchu. On a gorgeous morning atop Huayna Picchu, overlooking the ancient ruins in Machu Picchu, I proposed. Thankfully, Laura accepted, and the rest is history!

Laura loves me for who I am and not for what I have. Our needs are remarkably similar. We travel well together. She is the type of person who would sleep in a car with me in the middle of nowhere without much fuss, happy just because we are together. She comes from a loving, connected family and talks to her parents and siblings almost daily. Laura and her family have inspired me, showing me a version of family life I aim to achieve with my wife and daughter.

Laura's humble background and her humility is another thing I love about her. She grew up on a ranch in Mexico with no electricity or running water. The next ranch was about five miles away. She and her brother rode a horse to school and took bucket showers outside. They raised animals for food and ran around chasing chickens, playing with goats and pigs. The family ate what they had on the farm for meals, as this was a way of life. She has never been caught up in the materialism and hoopla of being an American with its sometimes selfish, entitled mentality.

Laura's nature is to build our relationship and take care of each other. Her desire to give more than she takes leads her to ask what she can do for me and our family instead of pushing for what she can get. I've been in other relationships where the demands on my time and the need for constant attention felt restrictive and controlling. Laura makes sure I remain grounded and humble, which is particularly important for me.

Laura's approach isn't passive or submissive. She has a calmness and strength about her. On a deep level, she understands the importance of personal space and time away from each other so we can bring 100% to the table when we are together. She's the opposite of needy, as if she operates on a higher level of self-confidence and surety. That's refreshing.

Her calm energy is a daily reminder to continue growing and working on myself to develop a deeper level of awareness and acceptance of who I am. By embracing a sense of calm and the inner peace that goes along with it, I transfer this energy to everyone around me, leading to better relationships and a greater acceptance of people. This helps me feel more genuine and authentic.

Mila is my second princess and daily inspiration. It's true what they say about children changing your life. Being there when Mila was born and experiencing the miracle of birth and everything that follows has profoundly changed my life in such an amazing, positive way. I am excited to be around Mila every day, holding her and making googly eyes with her. I can't wait to see her grow and to experience life through her eyes.

Fatherhood is like being a child all over again and has changed my perspective on life by shifting the focus even farther away from myself. Laura began this reshaping process, and Mila is taking it to a new level. I've learned when I shift my focus away from my own needs, I feel pure joy and a new depth of love in my heart. It's as if I have cleared space for more love to find its way inside me.

This shift has also revealed the power of letting go. Often, when you pursue something or someone, they elude you. When you let go of your own desires, wants, and need for control, the things you want show up in your life as if by magic.

Meeting Laura and going through the ordeal of her deportation and being apart from her for a year solidified my belief that love has no boundaries. Only people have boundaries. Most people set limits on other people and establish expectations. It's human nature, in some cases, necessary to keep our relationships with difficult people. The more offensive boundaries are the self-imposed limitations we set for ourselves. We limit how far we will go, what new experiences we are willing to try, and how much we are willing to give.

When Laura was battling with the immigration authorities, the depth of the interrogations and red tape was an endless nightmare. I learned my love truly has no boundaries. Especially the Mexican border.

Life Is about More Than Success

When I was younger, I believed making money, being wealthy, and receiving awards, accolades, and the approval and admiration of others was what success was all about. Climbing the corporate ladder, even if it means stepping on people below you, is what many people believe needs to happen to succeed. I believe being ruthless and being self-centered leads to unhappiness—with other people and within yourself.

I believe love is the answer and the cure for such thinking and behavior. Self-love is about maximizing your talents to the best of your ability and being the best you can be, not comparing yourself to others.

Being an inspiration to yourself and the people around you elevates everything you do and everyone you meet to higher levels. It's better to give than to get because the more you give, the more you get. If you want more, give more. We are all inspirational figures, and if we share our trials and experiences with each other, we can pull together and help each other. In sales, it's not unusual to meet people and consider how I might help them or to ask what I can get out of a given situation. Now, I feel much more interested in finding out about people and what's going on in their lives. If it turns out I can be of service, that's a bonus.

Emotional Mastery

Emotional mastery is essential for success. It helps us navigate the challenges of life and the bumps in the road when they appear. Without having a handle on our emotions, it is easy to spiral downward quickly when we feel overwhelmed. Having a solid mindset can turn a negative situation into a positive experience by shifting your focus and providing alternate perspectives.

Everything that happens during our days affects our emotions, creating the potential for emotional peaks and valleys. Having a powerful sense of emotional mastery allows us to operate and remain at peak performance and not experience an emotional roller coaster ride every time a new problem or challenge arises. Imagine emotional mastery as a smooth, horizontal line across the top of a graph versus a wavy line that starts at the top and heads to the bottom, then up again, down again.

As we've discussed in earlier chapters, one of the best skills you can develop is the ability to ask yourself and others open-ended questions that reveal alternative perspectives and ways of looking at situations. This can help when emotions are involved. Problems are a bad thing only if we perceive them as bad. By changing the way we perceive challenges and asking different, better questions, we can find solutions and consistently run at peak levels. We can also find ways to bring more balance into our lives. Deep down, most of us know what we need and want and how to get it. Take the time to have regular conversations with yourself to keep on track.

The best way to cultivate inner peace and true happiness is to build your life on a foundation of gratitude and thankfulness. Be thankful for each day because each one is truly a gift. Start and finish each day by saying thank you for all that you have. On tough days, realize that what you are experiencing is a wonderful day for other people; it's all a matter of perspective. Whether you see things as good or bad is truly up to you.

Most personal growth occurs when times are tough, not when things are going well. So, be thankful for every challenge. They are opportunities if you choose to look at them that way. So, welcome all challenges!

Keys:

- Take care of your physical and emotional health to create work/life balance.

- High energy = productivity and efficiency

- Be the engineer on your money train.

- Rejuvenate (vacations, other self-care)

- Start every day with a thank you.

 **Tools:**

Focus on gratitude for your blessings, and don't compare yourself to others.

It's more beneficial to be happy with what you have and with who you are than to continually pursue things you don't have or compare yourself to others. Although the grass might seem greener in your neighbor's yard, your neighbor might feel differently. They could be unhappy with their grass and feel hollow inside, despite their outward appearance. Who knows? As the old saying goes, "Don't judge books by their cover." Concentrate on our own blessings.

What are you grateful for today? You be you, and don't get caught up in comparisons.

Chapter 10

Carpe Diem

To hell with circumstances; I create opportunities.

Bruce Lee

Operating in seize-the-day mode is powerful, efficient, and leads to a high level of achievement and success. Working with this philosophy in business has served me well. My business has grown exponentially, my clients are happy, and I run my operations more efficiently than ever. No longer am I chasing my tail. But is carpe diem the right approach in all areas of life? Or all the time?

Some people run full throttle in every area of their life, checking items off their to-do lists at a feverish pace. This can work for a while, but there are costs associated with trying to seize every moment of every day. Burnout often happens quickly, and if you're always shooting for the moon, you miss many shining stars along the way.

I believe success is about the journey, not the destination. Coaching some very financially successful people, I've seen how easy it is to fall into the trap of making success and emotional fulfillment a moving target, always ahead of you, rather than enjoying the trip. This is a sure recipe for burnout.

Burnout occurs when we immerse ourselves in anything for too long without a break or change of scenery. Missing out on the joy of life's moments happens when we are so busy blazing through our days that we never stop to appreciate the little things while they are happening. We're either thinking about the past or planning for the future while we're in the present, missing the beauty and once-in-a-lifetime experiences happening now. The present moment is where life happens. The rest is anticipation and reflection.

I'm more of a go-with-the-flow type of guy, preferring to seize the day in the moments. Laura and I love to travel together, and Mila is already becoming a road warrior too. We enjoy going places without a plan or set itinerary and love variety and setting our own schedule, looking at a map, and hitting the road. When I'm on the road for business, I incorporate this same style. I love taking the back roads, exploring new places, and embracing the unpredictable.

Experience this for yourself by taking a different route on your way back and forth to work so you can see new things daily. I've always had a curious nature and embrace this side of my personality whenever possible, much the way I did when I was traveling around Europe on a shoestring budget after high school.

It's possible to seize the day and also be laidback, using a mix of styles to suit the situation. This gives you some options and mixes things up in your life. If you've set the bar high for your goals and desire to build your business or move up the ladder, then carpe diem needs to be a part of your approach. You're going to want to be active and organized to get where you want to go.

If you are an artist, your style might be more laid back and go-with-the-flow. Your casual nature might make your art special. You might not feel the need to run around and chase after every opportunity to get to the next level. You might view the seize-the-day crowd as rats in the giant rat race of life. That's totally fine.

What is most important is congruency between your current situation and style versus what you want and what you are willing to do to get there. If you are content living on a modest budget without too much focus on material goods and frills, then carpe diem is likely not so important. Perhaps you live in a small house that has a beautiful garden. A big house filled with modern technology wouldn't make you happy because you enjoy spending your days out in the garden. You are happy and perfectly content.

If you are unhappy, stressed, and constantly complaining because you are always struggling and wanting more than your small house can offer, then change your approach and up your game to meet more of your needs. Put yourself more consistently in an environment that is conducive to what you desire and want. Your current situation might reflect a go-with-the-flow style, but your needs and desires might demand a bit more carpe diem.

Overcoming Habitual Procrastination

Procrastination is a killer of progress regardless of your style and shows some form of fear or uncertainty. If you're sitting on the fence, you must ask yourself why. What's holding you back? What does it cost you by sitting on the fence, watching opportunities pass you by? At the very least, questions like these will be learning opportunities.

Analyze your pain—what's it costing you or perhaps

someone else when you don't do what you said you would do or what you can do? It's incredible how capable we are at getting comfortable with a certain amount of pain in our lives. The more pain we get used to, the less likely we will make a move. Procrastination continues. So, what do you do?

If your pain is not enough to tip the scales, focus on the pain you might be causing the people you love. When I am slacking or procrastinating, and I'm feeling perfectly fine being lazy, I think about Laura and how I might be affecting her. Letting myself down is one thing, but I'm not as willing to do that to her. I feel the same about Mila, so I have added motivation now.

Raise the level of pain you feel when you're procrastinating by attaching higher value to the cost of not making a move. Every day you procrastinate costs you double. People aren't going to like you. You'll be left behind, and most of us don't want that. All these negatives push the pendulum toward deciding and finally taking action.

Whatever triggers you, amp it up. If being selfish is something you dislike in yourself, you'll be spurred into action faster by sharing your struggles with others and shining a light on this behavior of yours that you wish to change. This tends to be an effective way for many people to spur action. However, it focuses on the negative motivation of avoiding pain.

For years I was reluctant to let others know I had epilepsy because I was afraid others would think less of me. In hindsight, I see how selfish this was. Not letting other people know the truth deprived them of the opportunity to know me better and myself of the opportunity to inspire others in ways I didn't even consider. Now, I realize it is my obligation to show others with epilepsy or some other supposed hindrance that this label does not have to slow them down at all. They can still compete to be the best in their respective industries, lead a kickass life, and be the best versions of themselves day in and day out!

Raise the value of hitting your goal or getting the job done. Focus on the simplicity of doing so. Focusing on benefits and pleasure is a positive form of motivation, which I encourage you to practice whenever possible. By making it easier to just do it instead of procrastinating and overthinking, you'll find the motivation to get moving. You can sit there and argue about it indefinitely, but if you spent a fraction of that energy doing the work, the job will get done, probably in less time than arguing with yourself. Once again, it's your choice.

Procrastination takes effort and energy. Often, it doesn't seem that way, or you don't feel it consciously, but every day you put something off, it's working on you, subconsciously.

Just Do It

There is a tremendous advantage to acting, then recalibrating. Action is where the rubber meets the road, but it's not all go, go, go. You must take the time to recalibrate too.

Ready, Fire, Recalibrate (RFR)!

Let's say you are going to fire a gun. The three steps most people learn are: ready, aim, fire. This is a useful sequence; however, I suggest that a more proactive approach is ready, fire, recalibrate.

What throws many people off is aiming. For example, when one is holding a gun and aiming at a target, the longer you wait to fire, the more likely the gun will move because of the weight. A better approach is to get ready, prepare quickly, and fire almost at once. Then, recalibrate based on your result and fire again. The same is true for our actions. When we sit around too long without acting, our motivation tires. When we fire and miss, it's easy to step away from the target, saying we're not good enough to hit the mark. Recalibrate each time you take quick action and keep going to see better results every time.

It is important to analyze quickly after each effort, whether shooting a gun or living your daily life. Examine what went right and what did not. But don't get stuck in paralysis by analysis! Get back on the playing field and start shooting for your targets again as soon as possible.

I apply the same philosophy when I'm golfing. Though I am not a professional golfer by any means, I can periodically put together some respectable rounds when I keep consistent, focus, and follow my routine. I take a few practice swings and visualize where I want the ball to go. Then, I take my swing. Based on my result, I recalibrate for my next shot. This is more helpful on the driving range than on the course, but do you get the point? Don't get caught up in stagnation and overthinking, which leads to no action whatsoever. Recalibrating quickly and efficiently, based on prior results, and making small improvements that compound over the long term will lead to phenomenal results.

In business, I prepare by following the examples set by other sales leaders and modeling what works for them. When I give a presentation or do something for the first time, these observations are my homework, building my mental muscle, and giving me the confidence to make it happen for myself.

Once I have a result, regardless of how effective it was, I recalibrate. I examine what worked great first. Second, I ask what can be improved the next time. Knowing I can recalibrate is what helps me pull the trigger with confidence and continue to grow to new heights each year.

The key is to take the first step, moving forward regardless of the potential outcomes. Now you have a benchmark to work with, and you can improve, recalibrate, and then try again. This is a simple, yet critical, shift in perspective. Instead of feeling you must be perfect on your first try, which is incredibly stressful, shift your focus to the ease and efficiency of improving.

I was reminded of the usefulness of this approach when writing and editing this book. Most people have a story or many stories to tell. Sitting down and writing them takes a massive amount of energy. Before I began, a million thoughts ran through my head. *Where do I start? How will I sort out everything I want to say? How will I find the right words? Will my book be good? Who will read it? Will they like it?* The list of fears and uncertainties was endless, and they could have stopped the writing process before it even started.

I talked myself off the ledge by reminding myself that when you have something written, regardless of how good or bad it is, you can edit and shape the words, allowing the story to unfold and develop. Editing is much easier than writing because you already have a benchmark set up, something you can see. In effect, when you edit, you are recalibrating your story, and this keeps the process moving.

By routinely practicing RFR, no matter how small the task, you will develop your courage muscle. When it comes time to tackle something more challenging, you will be in a better place to move forward. It will be easier to do your homework and get prepared, so when the time comes, you can move to the edge and throw yourself into your task wholeheartedly. Your mind and body will follow. You'll live to see another day and have a point of reference the next time.

Action Speaks Louder Than Words.

Focus on action. Visualize yourself already doing what it is you are seeking to achieve. Planning is essential but put a limit on how long you will stay in this phase. Focus on movement, action, and taking the first step. Once you get started, it will be much easier to continue.

The Power of Delegating

By releasing control, delegating, and outsourcing certain activities, your time is freed up to devote to your top clients and priorities. Let someone else manage certain tasks. Have faith in others by delegating tasks that suck away your time. When I finally got up the courage to start doing this, trusting someone else to do the same quality job with the same care and attention to detail I would provide, my life changed dramatically.

If you're resisting the idea, your ego or a fear of loss of control is probably the obstacle. When we are used to doing things our way, we become emotionally attached to the process and outcomes. Explaining how to do things our way and training someone to take over requires time and effort. It might seem easier to keep doing things ourselves. I understand those feelings because I used to think that way too. But I also see objections as excuses.

At the root of all excuses is fear. Push past this fear by making changes incrementally and slowly. Let go of one piece of the puzzle at a time. Each time you do, you'll gain experience and confidence to do it repeatedly. Before long, you'll wonder how you ever managed everything in the first place!

Create Your Best Life

What do you genuinely want in life? What are the big dreams you had when you were a child? Maybe you saw yourself standing on top of a mountain with the golden ring, health and wealth, peace, and happiness in unlimited supply.

Did you stop dreaming on your way up the mountain? Often, we get out of school and start making choices that lock us onto a particular path, and before you know it, life seems to have passed us by. But it hasn't. Not yet.

I'm here to tell you that you can have it all. You can make your dreams come true no matter what stage of life you are in. It's all up to you.

Take risks. Love what you wish to promote. Be persistent and remember that nothing is impossible. Cultivate high energy because you will need it.

Success is not guaranteed. It comes at a price. You'll need a vision, a plan to reach your vision, hard work, discipline, resilience, and forward motion toward your goals. By applying the principles in this book—have a clear vision, set goals that are deeply meaningful to you, seek mentors, be positive, form the best habits, be disciplined and persistent, and hold yourself accountable—anything in this world is possible.

Please use the many tools and the inspiration I have supplied and use them as shortcuts to shave many years off the learning curve. Reach for what you want in life. I'm cheering you on!

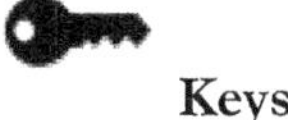

Keys:

- Learn to love deeply.
- Live with no regrets.
- Know that emotional fulfillment is the greatest gift in life.
- Follow your passions.
- Follow your heart.
- Seek happiness and fulfillment over money.

Tools:

Review your notebook and the notes you've taken as you read and completed various exercises in this book. If you skipped any, go back and complete them.

Review this list for reminders of the key points to consider on the road to success:

12 Keys to Success (The quick and easy guide!):

1. Attitude. A passionate attitude goes a long way

in the world. Effectively manage your state of being, using affirmations and visualization. Practice so your habitual nature becomes positive.

2. Goals. Goals should be done monthly, quarterly, and yearly. We can't hit and exceed targets we don't have. Goals should include a specific, vivid vision of what you want and clear whys. Ask yourself what you are willing to sacrifice to reach your goal. Be bold with your goals. Don't neglect to write your goals down. Review them continually (weekly) and share them with like-minded people so they can be consistently monitored and you can be held accountable.

   Set goals for all areas of your life. Be very descriptive of each goal and visualize with detail what each one looks like. For example, perhaps a 2019 Range Rover is on your goal list for the year. Visualize in detail the exterior color and outside curves of the vehicle, the color of the interior, and the exact interior options. What does the leather smell like as you drive it off the showroom floor? Are the tires bright and shiny with special rims? Is your favorite song coming from the custom sound system, making you smile? Use your senses to describe precisely, in detail, the car you want and manifest this vision coming to a reality. You just may surprise yourself when your goal comes to fruition.

3. Model and replicate. Find the best people in the business you are in and model and replicate what they are doing. Pick their brains, intern for them for free, be creative to get their attention, and earn their respect so you can gain time with them. Most people always want something in return for their work, but learning from the best for some months, even for no pay, is one of the best choices one can make. Observe what your mentor does differently from others. Model and replicate the behavior of those around you whom you admire most.

4. Dare to be different. If one thinks and does the same thing as most others, they will get average results. Take a different approach to be exceptional. Go a step above what others do.

Send personal, handwritten thank you cards and birthday cards. Most of your competition stick with emailed thank you notes. Think creatively to stand out. Strive to be in the top 1% in your field of endeavor while maintaining a tremendous life balance. Brainstorm other ways to set yourself apart from the average crowd.

5. CANI (constant and never-ending improvement). Education is ongoing. Attend peak performance training seminars and set aside a yearly budget for self-improvement. Can't afford the price of admission? Then volunteer! As staff, one often gets a behind-the-scenes look at training. You have the opportunity to give back and learn from the masters of performance. Make your car a traveling library. Stop listening to music all the time and listen to self-development audios and podcasts repetitively until they become part of your subconscious mind. Selectively choose a few podcasts that share great wisdom.

6. Mastermind and network. (LinkedIn, Facebook, Instagram, YouTube, Twitter) Use

social media to improve your business contacts. Don't pass up this new age of information; otherwise, the game of life will pass you by! LinkedIn is excellent for business contacts. Use it to enhance your network. Investigate other platforms to find one or two that work best for you and enhance various areas of your life.

7. Referrals. Most people love to feel like a hero and want to help others, so don't be shy and deprive them of this opportunity. Don't get caught up thinking this is just about you asking for referrals. Clients are people too. They enjoy helping others as much as you do. Simply ask, "If you are happy with my services, would you be so kind as to give me a few referrals?" Or perhaps, "I am selectively looking to expand my business to a few more clientele who would enjoy the same type of services I provide you. Who do you think might be interested?"

8. Ask internal, quality questions. The quality of one's life is directly reflective of the quality of questions they ask themselves. Empower yourself with great questions. We all have off

days. To snap out of a funk, ask yourself, "How can this serve me? How can I find appreciation in this challenge right now? What is the gift? What is it that I don't see?" Remember, every problem is a blessing in disguise if we learn from them. Challenges are there to serve us. We, and only we, decide what anything means, even the stuff we say to ourselves. We can immediately make sure any inner chatter gets programmed to serve us by asking empowering questions and shaping our own reality. This helps form a strong identity.

9. Rapport and relationship. Relationships are the most essential aspect of selling and life. Many people talk too much and never discover the needs of their customers. It's easy to talk yourself out of a sale but difficult to listen yourself out of a deal! Don't be pushy, as this will bite you in the long term. It might take multiple attempts to close a business transaction, and that is fine as this gives you more time to build a better, trusting relationship. When clients trust, the results will follow! Ask better quality questions to build

trust and rapport with others. Focus on the client and their needs, not your own. Apply the same principle to other relationships in your life.

10. Work/life/balance. Your sales will grow when you are laser-focused on the sales tasks at hand. Your life will grow when you focus on taking care of yourself. Take care of your health and eat right as this keeps your energy high and helps combat bummer days. Ask your peer group to keep you accountable. Your loved ones deserve the best of you and not the rest of you, so take time to rest your mind, body, and spirit consistently. Most everyone's performance rises when they are running on a full tank of energy instead of a half-depleted one.

11. Be Proactive. Winners anticipate while losers wait for the game of life to unfold and then react. The ability to anticipate and act quickly is enormously powerful. This is why young kids beat adults in video games predominantly; they can predict what lies in the road ahead. They

react accordingly and win. By being proactive and not reactive, and then quickly recalibrating based on your results, you will be way ahead with your results.

12. Never quit. Never assume a no from a client means never, and don't ever take a rejection personally. Don't burn bridges with a negative attitude. Think about the relationship overall. Put yourself in the shoes of your prospect to best strategize your approach and understand their needs. Remember to ask great questions. Be resilient and positive in all areas of your life.

Acknowledgments

I want to thank my wife Laura, who brings joy to my world every day. Her support helps me succeed in all areas of my life. She gives me space and autonomy to make things happen, encouraging me to steer my own ship. She's on board with my dreams and inspires me to take time for myself to rejuvenate my energy and my soul with projects like this one.

My mother, Marti McMahon Diamond, has made a solid imprint on my life, and I thank her and my stepfather Steve for their constant emotional support and advice.

I am grateful to my dad and my stepmom Kathy who are always up for a chat and are never shy about making sure I represent the McMahon lineage proudly and ethically. Thanks to them, my faith in God is strong.

Though my daughter Mila is a young toddler as I write

this, the pride and joy of her presence in my life was an inspiration for much of what I shared with you. Someday, she will read this and know how thankful I am to be her father.

I cannot thank my brother Derek and sister Danielle enough for doing whatever is necessary to bring our large extended families together. I can always depend on them to be there for the family, and I thank them for putting up with me throughout the years!

I also want to thank my editors, Michele and Ken Budka at Full Sail Publishing, for their friendship and guiding light. Without them, this book would never have happened.

To my many friends at McKesson (past and present) who have helped and inspired me over the years, especially Jeff Butler, John Sullivan, Brad Jacob, Tom Jacob, Mike Miller, Mark Vukelich, Dustin Brister, Kevin O'Regan, Keith Cony, Thomas Page, Imran Mahzar, Richie Mitchell, Craig Dahl, Steve Reas, Mark Fitch, Penny Mulder, Brian Valley, Sean Nelson, Gary Corless, Paul Julian, Eddie Dienes, Gary Keeler, John Hammergren, and Brian Tyler…thank you.

For my friends at the Tony Robbins Organization, most notably the volunteer staff and crew, leadership, my fellow trainers, and of course, Tony himself, thank you! Together we have served alongside each other for many years. I have learned so much from you, and I am forever grateful. Special thank you to head trainers Tad Schinke and Vicki St George for all your tremendous support over the years.

Thank you also to Steve Linder (founder of Strategic Brain), who was fundamental to my understanding and application of neuro-linguistic programming (NLP) in my everyday life and in business.

To Joe Williams for helping me become a better speaker…thank you!

I am grateful to many other life-long friends for supporting my dreams since I was a teenager. Most notably Andrew Blair, Mark Uyemoto, David Timberlake, Bruce Triplett, Terry Ho, Tom Fahres, Malinda Grumblatt, Rossana Broll, Derek Carlson, Jeff Montague, Marty Munn, Rajeev, and Sunny Chopra.

I also owe the late Paul Steven's (Coach) and my grandfather (Papa) a huge debt of gratitude for supporting and molding my competitive desires and spirits through sports. They taught me nothing was impossible with desire, grit, focus, and vision!

Cheers to all my GoBundance mastermind friends, most notably Mark Schwaiger, Sam Wegert, Rock Thomas, Daniel Del Real, Mike McCarthy, Aaron West, Tim Rhode, Daniel Ramsey, David Osborn, Mario Mazzamuto, Doug Lambert, Andrew Cushman, Pat Hiban, Jeremy Reisig, Dirk van Reenen, Jon Berghoff, Steven Hatcher, and Diego Corzo.

Finally, thank you to my friends and fellow life strategist partners, Chuck Hogan and Tony Rodrigues. Let's continue to inspire one soul at a time and truly make an impact in this world!

About the Author

Darren McMahon was blessed to have had his life spared after a decades-long battle with epilepsy and has devoted himself to inspiring others to pursue their goals and dreams. As a sales professional, he has generated over 100 million dollars in sales during his career as a perennial, award-winning, top sales executive for the fortune eight company McKesson. Darren has been deeply involved in the personal development arena for the past twenty years. He is an international trainer, peak performance strategist, and speaker who has touched thousands of lives. He has repeatedly beaten the odds and inspires others to cherish their battles, as well as their triumphs.

Made in the USA
Middletown, DE
11 May 2021

39474618R00166